IMAGES
of America

MARCH OF DIMES

BASIL O'CONNOR, 1957. Daniel Basil O'Connor (1892–1972), known affectionately to his friends as "Doc," was the first president of the National Foundation for Infantile Paralysis (now known as the March of Dimes), serving from 1938 to 1972. A graduate of Dartmouth College and Harvard Law School, he partnered with Franklin Delano Roosevelt to conquer poliomyelitis, first at the Georgia Warm Springs Foundation and subsequently as president of the National Foundation. Basil O'Connor's foremost achievement was the leadership of a public fundraising crusade—the March of Dimes—based on the philanthropy of common people and the coordination of a massive medical research effort that led to the creation of the Salk vaccine, which was field tested in 1954. He was a masterful, savvy, results-oriented leader, adept at using modern mass-communication media to promote the work of the National Foundation. Astutely aware of the historic role of the foundation, he created its Historical Division, which worked from 1953 to 1957 to document meticulously the events leading up to the vaccine and field trial.

IMAGES
of America
MARCH OF DIMES

David W. Rose

ARCADIA

First printed in 2003.

Published by Arcadia Publishing,
an imprint of Tempus Publishing Inc.
2A Cumberland Street
Charleston, SC 29401

Printed in Great Britain.

Library of Congress Catalog Card Number: 2003106545

For all general information, contact Arcadia Publishing:
Telephone 843-853-2070
Fax 843-853-0044
E-mail sales@arcadiapublishing.com

For customer service and orders:
Toll-free 1-888-313-2665

Visit us on the Internet at www.arcadiapublishing.com.

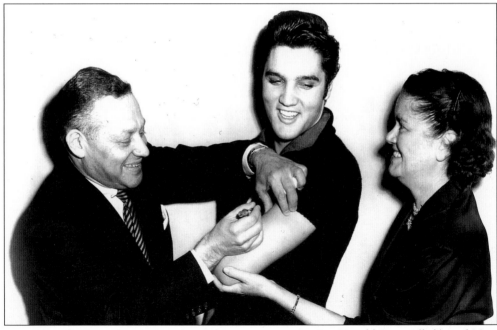

THE ELVIS PRESLEY INOCULATION, OCTOBER 28, 1956. Dr. Harold Fuerst (left) and New York City health commissioner Leona Baumgartner administer a polio vaccination to Elvis Presley in the National Foundation's Teens Against Polio publicity efforts. Calling Presley "the Pied Piper of modern youth," the foundation distributed the photograph in a flyer to more than 600 Elvis fan clubs across the nation to encourage teenage polio vaccinations.

CONTENTS

ACKNOWLEDGMENTS

It is my sincere pleasure to offer thanks to several individuals who have provided critical assistance with this project. First and foremost, I wish to thank Jennifer Coate for her generosity in sharing with me the breadth of her knowledge and all the photographic resources of the foundation. Since 1992, Jennifer has served as chief photographer for the March of Dimes. She and her predecessors have created this photographic record, and March of Dimes history is all the richer for it. John Blecha was chief photographer from 1949 to 1990, and his work forms the lion's share of the photographs to be found herein. Blecha founded the Photography Department of the National Foundation for Infantile Paralysis in 1945 and photographed events of the polio vaccine field trial and much more. Douglas Ogawa served as assistant photographer (1970–1985) and Brian Douglas as chief photographer (1988–1992). I salute them all for their artistry and achievements in documenting an essential part of American history.

William Stock, director of the Audiovisual Division, provided critical guidance and stimulating ideas every step of the way. He and Peter Coletta are always generous with their time and knowledge about our film and video collections. Dr. Jennifer L. Howse, March of Dimes president, and Jane Massey, chief operating officer and executive vice president, have been instrumental in their support not only of this project but also of the creative utilization of all our archival resources. Beverly Robertson continually provides upbeat advice and encouragement; it is a distinct pleasure to work under Beverly's direction. I wish to extend my sincere thanks to Doug Staples, Dr. Michael Katz, Stephanie Harwood, Kathy D'Aloise, Dick Leavitt, and Lori Schulman for their expert recommendations on language, content, style, and March of Dimes protocol. Any errors of fact or infelicities of phrase herein are strictly mine, and not theirs.

My predecessor at the March of Dimes, Jane Gorjevsky, now curator of the Carnegie Collections at the Rare Book and Manuscript Library of Columbia University, set the groundwork for this project by her meticulous organization of the polio-era photographs and creation of a searchable database. I extend my thanks also to Bob Aglione, Janis Biermann, Barbara Blume, Christine Convey, Terri Creeden, Mike Finnerty, Ellen Fiore, Lynda Knight, Mark Roithmayr, Mary-Elizabeth Reeve, Albert Rosenfeld, Hope Ryan, Frank Vitale, Wendy Scott-Williams, Robin Wexler, and Lindsay Whitcomb for their assistance with many details. Special thanks go to L.J. Coulthurst for information about aviation and sports. My work as archivist is always enjoyable thanks to all my colleagues of the Education and Health Promotion Division and especially those of the Pregnancy & Newborn Health Education Center.

To Sue Rose, my wife and director of program services of the March of Dimes Greater New York Chapter, I owe a huge debt of gratitude. Her critical acumen, keen sense of detail, and knowledge of March of Dimes programs and issues have kept me right on track. I particularly enjoyed our many evenings discussing the work in progress. Thanks also to my father-in-law, James B. Brucks, a native New Yorker, who helped identify several New York City locations. Finally, thanks to Phil Schaap of WKCR radio of Columbia University in New York City for assistance with the photograph of Louis Armstrong.

INTRODUCTION

The biologist Edward O. Wilson has remarked that a society is defined not only by what it creates but also by what it chooses *not* to destroy. That these photographs exist at all is a testament to individuals with foresight (among them is Basil O'Connor) who have wisely chosen to preserve the history that they themselves created. That this photographic retrospective is published now is a function of a particular moment when the value of history has vastly increasing importance and the field of archival studies grows exponentially. Our expanded awareness of the exigencies of preservation impels us to the necessity of education.

With this photographic history, the March of Dimes hopes to present the enduring legacy of its role in American society as it steps forward in 2003 with a new campaign against the epidemic of premature birth. These images have been selected from the many thousands in the March of Dimes Archives to highlight the significant accomplishments and turning points in the foundation's history. Through this small fraction of the total collection, one may glimpse not only the contours but also the essence of the program of the March of Dimes to eradicate polio. The photographs also vividly portray the foundation's transformation in the post-polio era into a leader in the fight against birth defects and infant mortality.

The intensive study of photographs changes one's relationship to them. Careful and concentrated study leads to greater intimacy with the photograph subjects, opening the eye of memory and providing opportunities for reflection and wonder. I invite you to bring a heightened quality of awareness to these captivating photographs, to ponder them with care. The photographs are captivating because they are about people. Very often they are also about human suffering—in this case, poliomyelitis and birth defects. The March of Dimes has always understood that documenting these afflictions requires an ethics of perception. We bear witness to individual vulnerabilities only because we are so decisively committed to overthrow through science and education what the camera records. In the final analysis, often what the camera has recorded will be uplifting because the momentous struggle to overcome disease and disability demands the enrichment of shared experience and the binding ties of collective effort.

War and peace, epidemic disease, scientific and technological revolution, the American spirit of volunteerism, and the quest to construct a society of justice and fairness—all these themes will be found here as central to the story. The March of Dimes story is itself central to American history. It is a story that in its public dimensions is sometimes noisy with eager publicity and self-promotion, and for good reasons. However, as George Eliot reflected in the final sentences of *Middlemarch*, "the growing good of the world is partly dependent on unhistoric acts." "Unhistoric acts" are the personal, individual, everyday acts that so often go unnoticed as if they are completely lost to history—acts of love, service, sacrifice, and common philanthropy. You will find them here in abundance, for they have not been lost. They have been preserved in these photographs as the most compelling part of an incredible story.

ELAINE WHITELAW AND HELEN HAYES, NOVEMBER 1951. Elaine Whitelaw (left) was for many years the National Foundation's director of women's activities. A Smith College graduate, she joined the foundation in 1942 and quickly attained a commanding role at the forefront of the struggle against polio. Whitelaw's talent for empowering women in chapter and state leadership was instrumental in the national development of volunteers and in the complex logistics of the Salk vaccine field trial. Here, she poses with Helen Hayes at a women's conference in Boston, Massachusetts. Hayes also had an unparalleled role with the National Foundation. An inspiring actress of stage and screen, celebrated as "First Lady of the American Theater," she devoted her life to defeating polio after her daughter, Mary MacArthur, died from the disease in 1949. Hayes became national chairwoman of women's activities (1949–1961) and National Mothers March chairwoman (1951–1961), never tiring of encouraging polio patients and promoting the March of Dimes. The prize-winning poster in the background, *Polio Research—A Light Is Beginning to Dawn* (1949), was done by Herbert Bayer for the Museum of Modern Art.

One

THE EARLY YEARS

Poliomyelitis was one of the most feared illnesses of the 20th century. A contagious viral disease, it was known as infantile paralysis, or simply polio. It brought on symptoms as inconsequential as a headache and sore throat or as devastating as respiratory paralysis and death. Poliovirus destroys motor nerve cells of the spinal cord and brain stem, often leading to severe and usually permanent paralysis. Franklin Delano Roosevelt (FDR), undoubtedly polio's most famous victim, contracted it as an adult and never recovered the use of his legs. Roosevelt had the greatest social impact on the history of the disease. While president of the United States, he founded the National Foundation for Infantile Paralysis.

The National Foundation for Infantile Paralysis officially began its existence on January 3, 1938, though it was preceded by three organizations centering on the polio mission. The first was the Georgia Warm Springs Foundation, established in 1927 by FDR as a patient care center. Georgia Warm Springs was a therapeutic haven for polio sufferers, and its association with the president brought it wide renown. The second was the Committee for the Celebration of the President's Birthday, launched in 1934 to raise money, through public celebrations of FDR's birthday, to finance the costs of polio patient care nationwide. The third predecessor organization was the President's Birthday Ball Commission for Infantile Paralysis Research, which awarded funds raised by the birthday ball committee to medical researchers to learn more about the dreaded disease.

The original mission of the National Foundation was "to lead, direct, and unify the fight" against polio. In essence, the National Foundation efficiently consolidated the functions of its three predecessors by directly financing patient care and medical research through regular fundraising campaigns. To this, it added professional education programs to augment patient care. The foundation's president, Basil O'Connor, sparked a further innovation; from its headquarters in New York City, the foundation inaugurated a dynamic system of local chapters to coordinate the fight against polio in nearly every county of the United States. The difficulties of the early years were compounded in the 1940s by World War II, which drained the resources of both the nation and the new foundation, just as the severity and frequency of polio epidemics began to climb.

Historian Saul Benison has best summarized the situation the foundation faced in its early years:

> In 1937 . . . President Roosevelt became convinced that polio could only be conquered through a broad and sustained program of scientific education and research. The organization of the National Foundation for Infantile Paralysis was in essence the first step toward the realization of that goal. It was also something more. At a time when deadly assaults had already been launched against the human spirit and life itself in Europe, the new Foundation . . . stood as an affirmation of the value of conserving human life and dignity. Ordinary people everywhere recognized this quality and quietly and emphatically made its cause their own.

Indeed, the new foundation soon became a beloved institution, best known through its fundraising campaign, the March of Dimes.

FRANKLIN D. ROOSEVELT AT GEORGIA WARM SPRINGS, C. THE 1930S. Eleanor Roosevelt stands with Basil O'Connor and FDR at poolside of the glass-enclosed pool of the Georgia Warm Springs Foundation. The foundation was a nonprofit medical institution organized by FDR in 1927. Personally impressed by the rehabilitative effects of the naturally warm waters of the spring that had attracted vacationers since the 1890s, Roosevelt purchased the Warm Springs resort to transform it into an after-care treatment center for polio victims.

A CLASSROOM, GEORGIA WARM SPRINGS, C. 1930. Basil O'Connor served as treasurer and chairman of the executive committee of the Georgia Warm Springs Foundation and succeeded FDR as its president. Later, the National Foundation awarded grants and funded building projects at Warm Springs, such as the construction of the Roosevelt Hall rehabilitation center. Local March of Dimes chapters financed patient care. After 1941, the foundation established postgraduate education programs in physical and occupational therapy.

THE BRACE SHOP, GEORGIA WARM SPRINGS, C. THE 1930S. This is a general view of the brace shop where braces and prosthetic devices were designed and constructed based on specifications for each individual patient. Horace H. Maddox (left), director and chief brace maker, works on a leg brace while Russell Glenn molds a midsection support.

THE GEORGIA HALL BUILDING FUND, 1933. Arthur Carpenter (left) receives a check representing the proceeds of an auction sale of a bale of cotton to benefit the Georgia Hall Building Fund at Georgia Warm Springs. FDR appointed Arthur Carpenter, a former advertising manager for *Parents' Magazine*, as Georgia Warm Springs's business manager. Originally a polio patient in 1928, Carpenter attracted his friend, Keith Morgan, to the foundation as fundraising director. The two men on the right are unidentified.

A Dinner at Warm Springs, c. the 1930s. This photograph, from a personal collection of Basil O'Connor, depicts a dinner at Georgia Warm Springs with President Roosevelt and his associates. To the far left, an attendant plays the accordion. Seated, from left to right, are an unidentified person, Bernard Baruch (financier and presidential advisor), Basil O'Connor, Pres. Franklin D. Roosevelt, actress Bette Davis, and Adm. William D. Leahy.

A Birthday Party for Franklin D. Roosevelt, 1931. The president blows out the candles at a birthday celebration at Meriweather Inn in Georgia Warm Springs. Eleanor Roosevelt stands on the left. In 1934, the Committee for the Celebration of the President's Birthday was organized to raise funds to fight infantile paralysis with "birthday ball" celebrations. The committee's slogan was "Dance, so that others may walk." The committee remained prominent in the fundraising activities of the National Foundation through the war years.

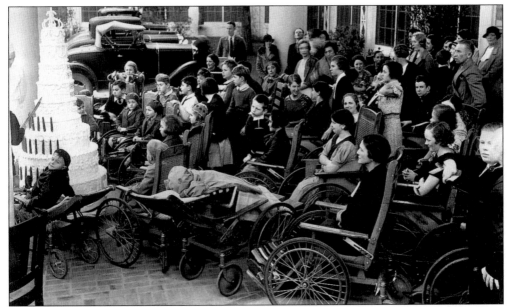

THE PRESIDENT'S BIRTHDAY, GEORGIA WARM SPRINGS, C. 1935. Patients observe the cutting of FDR's birthday cake. FDR was enormously popular at Georgia Warm Springs, and his birthdays were celebrated with enthusiasm and delight. Here, the president relaxed and formed affectionate associations with little of the formality of high office, winning the admiration and enjoying the camaraderie of young and old alike who shared his disability.

THE PRESIDENT'S BIRTHDAY BALL, 1936. The tradition of using FDR's birthday (January 30) for nationwide fundraising dances also led to the creation of the President's Birthday Ball Commission for Infantile Paralysis Research. FDR appointed the bacteriologist Paul de Kruif, author of *The Microbe Hunters* (1926), secretary to the commission, which funded research on polio prevention. The commission was the direct precursor of the National Foundation for Infantile Paralysis, founded in 1938.

THE ANTI-PARALYSIS CAMPAIGN, OCTOBER 25, 1938. The Committee for the Celebration of the President's Birthday and the National Foundation for Infantile Paralysis customarily sought FDR's sanction for using his birthday for fundraising each year. Seated, from left to right, are President Roosevelt; Keith Morgan, campaign committee chairman; George E. Allen, campaign director; Joseph M. Schenck, vice chairman; Basil O'Connor; and George W. Baker Jr., state leader.

A RADIO BROADCAST, DECEMBER 7, 1939. Basil O'Connor (left) and Keith Morgan (center) appear here with NBC newscaster Lowell Thomas in an early appeal for funds for the March of Dimes. O'Connor's use of the radio medium led to the creation of the Radio, Television, and Motion Picture Department of the National Foundation, directed by Howard J. London.

FUNDRAISING CAMPAIGN TOTALS, 1941. Keith Morgan and Basil O'Connor (both on the right) display to FDR the results of the 1941 fundraising campaign of the National Foundation for Infantile Paralysis, led by the Committee for the Celebration of the President's Birthday. Morgan was the fundraising director of the Georgia Warm Springs Foundation and national chairman of the birthday ball committee. On the lower right, he inscribed the original photograph, "To Doc, Friend, mentor pal—a warm hearted human dynamo."

POLIO RESEARCH, 1941. Basil O'Connor directs a meeting of his key medical advisors. Dr. Donald W. Gudakunst (left) was the National Foundation's first medical director until his untimely death in 1945. Dr. Morris Fishbein, editor of the *Journal of the American Medical Association*, became a close personal advisor to O'Connor. Dr. Thomas M. Rivers (right), a leading virologist, was chairman of the National Foundation's Committee on Virus Research.

THE GREATER NEW YORK CHAPTER FUNDS, C. 1943. The National Foundation's Greater New York Chapter distributes $49,000 to city hospitals at the office of Mayor Fiorello LaGuardia (center). Among those present are, from left to right, Lewis J. Valentine, police commissioner; D. Walker Wear, the National Foundation; Patrick Walsh, fire commissioner; Almerindo Portfolio, city treasurer; Keith Morgan; Basil O'Connor; Dr. Leo Mayer; and George L. Shearer, New York Foundation chairman.

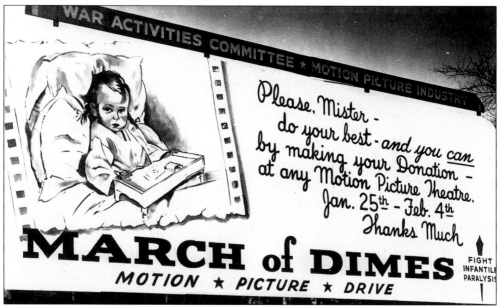

MOTION PICTURE DRIVE, C. 1943. During the war years, the motion picture industry supported the March of Dimes with a dime collection program in movie theaters nationwide. The War Activities Committee of the motion picture industry sanctioned and organized this activity. Though war news and concerns eclipsed the impact of advertising messages, movie theater collections greatly strengthened the foundation's revenue.

AMERICA'S SWEETHEART, JANUARY 10, 1944. Mary Pickford, a star of silent films and widely known as "America's Sweetheart," appears here with O'Connor in Grand Central Station. Pickford, one of the most popular and powerful women in the history of cinema, was the National Foundation's first national chairperson of women's activities (1947–1948). Her films included *Poor Little Rich Girl* (1917), *Rebecca of Sunnybrook Farm* (1917), and *Pollyanna* (1920). (Courtesy of the Metropolitan Photograph Service.)

MARY PICKFORD NATIONAL TOUR, JANUARY 1944. Mary Pickford and Basil O'Connor collect money in a giant top hat during her 1944 fundraising tour for the National Foundation. Other stops included a White House luncheon with Eleanor Roosevelt, christening of the ship *Samnid* at Baltimore's Bethlehem-Fairfield Shipyard, and visits to children's and army hospitals in Shreveport, Dallas, St. Louis, Indianapolis, and Cleveland.

A Human Blood Bank in Luzon, c. 1944. Basil O'Connor visits Luzon, Philippine Islands, on a tour of American Red Cross installations in the Pacific. He is discussing with operators of a mobile blood bank the details of supplying whole blood gathered in the States to war casualties at the front. FDR appointed O'Connor chairman of the American Red Cross in 1944, and he served in this capacity until 1949, while simultaneously holding the presidency of the National Foundation. (Courtesy of the American Red Cross.)

Somewhere in Northern France, 1945. Lt. Gen. George Patton and Basil O'Connor discuss Red Cross activities by the general's "three-star" jeep in the closing year of the war. O'Connor also regularly visited wounded soldiers in military hospitals when he toured the front, and his experiences with the logistics of medical operations during the war were invaluable in later national efforts at home against polio. (Courtesy of the American Red Cross.)

THE TIMES SQUARE MOTION PICTURE DRIVE, 1945. This advertising façade in Times Square for the March of Dimes fundraising drive in 1945 was associated with the motion picture War Activities Committee. The National Foundation gradually moved away from the president's birthday balls in the last years of the war, while the annual March of Dimes fundraiser during these years emphasized patriotism and national defense.

HARRY S. TRUMAN AND BASIL O'CONNOR, JANUARY 30, 1945. O'Connor inscribed this photograph at the lower left, "To Harry S. Truman Vice-President with many thanks from Basil O'Connor." O'Connor received Truman's continued support for the National Foundation program after President Roosevelt's death and later served as president of the Harry S. Truman Library in Independence, Missouri.

19

THE DEATH OF PRESIDENT ROOSEVELT, APRIL 12, 1945. Patients at Georgia Warm Springs read about Pres. Franklin D. Roosevelt's death in front of Georgia Hall. An event that shocked a world extremely weary of war, the death of FDR meant not only a wartime change of the United States commander in chief but also the loss of a beloved and familiar national leader whose life was a constant inspiration to polio victims and the disabled.

THE DEAN OF AMERICAN VIROLOGISTS, MARCH 13, 1946. Comdr. Thomas M. Rivers of the U.S. Naval Reserve was director of the hospital of the Rockefeller Institute for Medical Research. Rivers was known as "the Dean of American Virologists." Here he discusses polio research with Basil O'Connor during a National Foundation Medical Advisory Committee meeting at the Waldorf-Astoria Hotel in New York City. During the war, Rivers helped establish the Naval Medical Research Unit No. 2 in the Pacific. (Courtesy of Raymond K. Martin.)

THE MARCH OF DIMES, 1946. Actor Douglas Fairbanks Jr. points to a calendar marking the start of the 1946 March of Dimes. The March of Dimes was originally an annual January event so central to fundraising for polio that it became identified in the public mind with the National Foundation itself. Fairbanks, a naval officer during the war, starred in the film classics *The Prisoner of Zenda* (1937), *Gunga Din* (1939), and *Sinbad the Sailor* (1947).

AN EMERGENCY IN BUCHAREST, NOVEMBER 17, 1945. Rev. Vasile Hatigan, rector of the St. Dumitru's Romanian Orthodox Church, bestows his blessing on an iron lung and the airplane about to fly it from LaGuardia Airport to Bucharest, Romania. Airport scenes like this became all too familiar in the 1950s as the National Foundation responded to national and international needs for air transport of iron lungs and patients.

FIGHTING IN THE DARK, C. 1941. Artist McClelland Barclay poses with his painting *Fighting in the Dark* for the National Foundation. Barclay's artwork appeared on magazine covers such as the *Saturday Evening Post*. A hallmark of his art was renditions of stunningly beautiful women, and General Motors commissioned Barclay illustrations for an advertisement campaign with the slogan "Body by Fisher." A lieutenant commander in the U.S. Naval Reserve, Barclay also designed camouflage for U.S. fighter planes and painted portraits for the navy. He was listed as missing in action after his LST (landing ship tank) was torpedoed in the Pacific in 1943. McClelland Barclay's *Fighting in the Dark* is a vivid emblem of the early years of the National Foundation for Infantile Paralysis. For the first decade of its existence, the foundation faced the predicament of fighting polio in one of the darkest times of modern history. Though another decade of polio epidemics lay ahead, there would soon be light to quell this darkness.

Two

EPIDEMIC POLIO: CRISIS AND RESPONSE

The first known polio epidemic in the United States, relatively small and localized, occurred in central Vermont in 1894. The epidemic of 1916, however, was devastating; striking hard in New York City, polio cases outnumbered the physicians and facilities for adequate treatment, and panic ensued. Little was known about the disease apart from its crippling effects, and for years, public health authorities could do no more than initiate common-sense hygienic measures as medical doctors continued to treat the disease symptomatically.

The National Foundation for Infantile Paralysis entered the scene in 1938, just as polio was again on the rise. The foundation funded advanced medical research that ultimately brought answers about polio prevention, but in the short run, it was direct aid to individuals and communities that was needed most desperately. At a time when comprehensive medical and hospital insurance was not available, a polio case requiring hospitalization and prolonged aftercare could stretch a family's resources beyond the breaking point. The foundation stepped in to pay all expenses for patients, saving countless families from bankruptcy.

However, financial aid awards to polio patients and their families were only part of the foundation's comprehensive program to provide the most effective response to the complex realities of epidemics. Medical services of the National Foundation included epidemic preparedness measures that were coordinated with state and local health departments; emergency relief in the form of medical supplies, equipment, and even the construction of hospital facilities; and the recruitment, training, and dispatch of professional and lay personnel to communities in need. The foundation organized a cadre of non-technical volunteers called Polio Emergency Volunteers to assist medical staff in hospitals, aftercare centers, and in the field. It organized Epidemic Aid Units of nurses, physical therapists, and medical social workers. It financed respiratory treatment facilities and purchased, stockpiled, and transported iron lungs, ultimately creating regional respiratory equipment centers. It developed nursing, occupational therapy, and psychological services for polio victims. Its programs were wide-ranging but tailored to specific crises.

In the years of World War II shortages, Basil O'Connor's personal methodology was to ask an affected community, "What do you have, and what do you need?" This nuts-and-bolts approach was the basis for a sophisticated chapter-and-volunteer-response system to polio epidemics for more than 20 years. The foundation also capitalized on the spectacular nature of polio epidemics to publicize its mission, leading to a grassroots revolution in fundraising. The painful momentum of each epidemic was an opportunity for both relief and solicitation, for it was an all-out war against a disease.

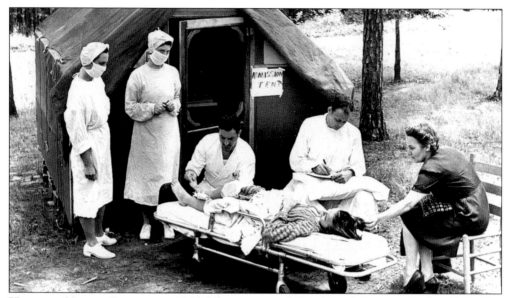

HICKORY, NORTH CAROLINA, 1944. The summer of 1944 brought a severe and sudden polio epidemic to western North Carolina. Charlotte Memorial Hospital in the little city of Hickory (Catawba County) found itself with a flood of young children stricken with polio, more than it could handle, and the National Foundation stepped forward with emergency assistance. Here, physicians examine a girl on a portable cot at an admission tent near an emergency hospital erected to handle the crisis.

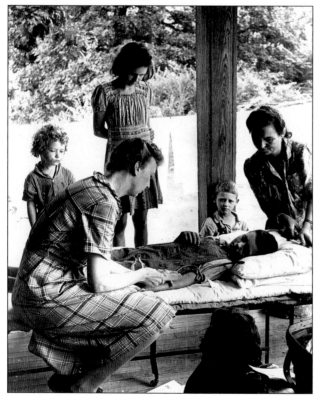

THE MIRACLE OF HICKORY, 1944. Within a matter of weeks, the National Foundation Catawba County Chapter coordinated a relief effort in Hickory to bring swift medical action to the afflicted region. Days later, a functioning emergency hospital was erected and equipped. The foundation touted the story—the Miracle of Hickory—as a model of successful epidemic response. Here, Dr. Dorothy Horstmann of Yale University Medical School, a grantee of the National Foundation, draws a blood sample.

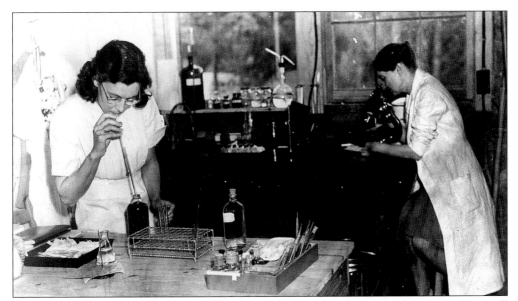

EMERGENCY INFANTILE PARALYSIS HOSPITAL, 1944. This is an interior view of a small laboratory installed at the Emergency Infantile Paralysis Hospital in Hickory. By November, the National Foundation had sent nearly $400,000 in emergency aid, from March of Dimes funds, to North Carolina. While epidemic response in Hickory seemed nothing short of miraculous, with 68 percent of patients fully recovered, the National Foundation would be challenged continually in the coming years with similar scenarios across the country.

THE FIELD SERVICE UNIT, OCTOBER 1946. The National Foundation's nine-ton, mobile field unit debuted as an emergency service provider for polio patients at St. Francis Hospital in Peoria, Illinois. Equipped with a respirator, hot-pack machine, resuscitation unit, and self-contained power generator, it served as a mobile classroom and clinic, as well as an emergency transport device. From Peoria, the field unit traveled to Ithaca, New York, and then to Baltimore Children's Hospital with a respirator patient. Its use was discontinued in the early 1950s.

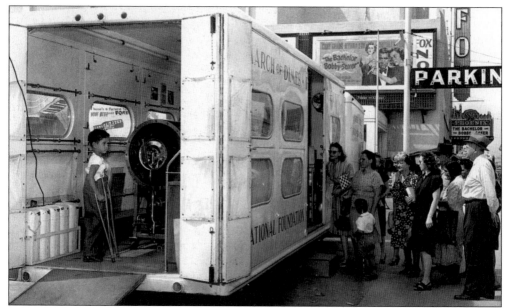

THE FIELD SERVICE UNIT, OCTOBER 1, 1947. This is a partial interior view of the mobile field unit parked on location in Phoenix, Arizona. The boy standing onboard is Martin Pavell, whose case was handled by the Greater New York Chapter from 1944 until 1947, when his family relocated to Phoenix. Martin appeared in the 1948 March of Dimes campaign for the Maricopa Chapter of the National Foundation in Arizona.

THE NEW YORK RECONSTRUCTION HOME, APRIL 1947. Physical therapist Mary Eleanor Brown instructs patients on how to use crutches in a supine position at the New York Reconstruction Home in West Haverstraw, New York. The National Foundation provided direct financial assistance to individual polio patients and their families for physical therapy as well as for hospital care, nursing, vocational rehabilitation, transportation to treatment centers, and other medical services. (Courtesy of Raymond K. Martin.)

A Clinical Lecture, 1951. Dr. Robert L. Bennett, director of physical medicine at the Georgia Warm Springs Foundation, demonstrates the function and positioning of a corset and neck brace to a class of staff and student physiotherapists. March of Dimes funds eventually supported a wide-ranging professional educational program at Georgia Warm Springs and other medical institutions throughout the United States.

The Polio Emergency Volunteers, June 1955. The National Foundation launched its Polio Emergency Volunteer (PEV) program in 1945 to train lay people to assist physicians, nurses, and physical therapists. American Red Cross nurses' aides were a model for the program and the key group from which volunteers were drawn. Here, respiratory patient Wilma Wampler speaks with PEV Kitty Wheatley at the Southwestern Respiratory Center in Houston, Texas.

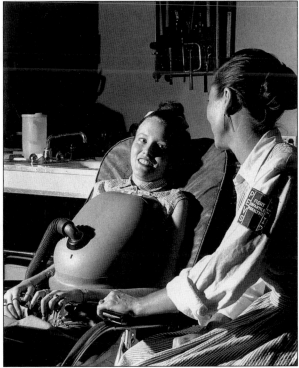

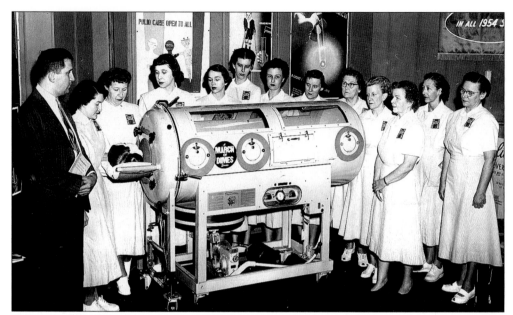

PEVs and the Iron Lung, 1954. Polio Emergency Volunteers of Daviess County, Kentucky, are shown here with an iron-lung exhibit during the 1954 March of Dimes. Standing at the left is Dr. J. Edmund Bickel, who taught part of the PEV course. The National Foundation Women's Division, under the leadership of Elaine Whitelaw, was responsible for administering the PEV program. (Courtesy of the Owensboro Messenger.)

The Role of Nurses, October 1955. Alice Kimball Fales, who volunteered to work with polio patients after her retirement from nursing, reads to a young boy at Haynes Memorial Hospital in Boston, Massachusetts. The National Foundation supported the nursing profession extensively through direct grants, aid to nursing centers, training programs, publications, scholarships, and fellowships.

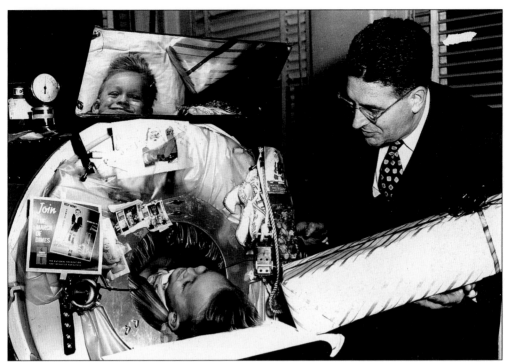

SAVED BY THE IRON LUNG, 1953. Barret Hoyt, the first polio patient saved by an iron lung (in 1929), delivers a Christmas gift to three-year-old James Robinson at Haynes Memorial Hospital in Boston. To bring some comfort to iron-lung patients, it became traditional for family and friends to attach greeting cards, artwork, toys, family photographs, March of Dimes literature, and other decorations to the collar area of the respirator, as seen in this photograph.

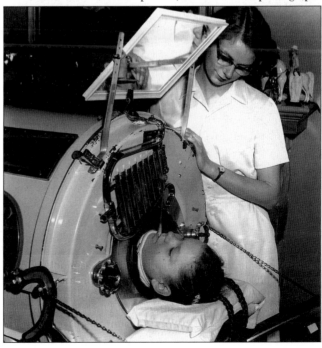

TO PLAY A GLOCKENSPIEL, SEPTEMBER 1957. An example of the determination of iron-lung patients is illustrated here in young Carol Hicks of Wapakoneta, Ohio, who plays a glockenspiel (mounted on her iron lung) with a mouth-held mallet. Note the home environment with porcelain statuettes on the mantelpiece in the background. Carol played the U.S. Marine Corps hymn on her glockenspiel in the March of Dimes film *Survival Is Not Enough* (1958).

A FAMILY IN CRISIS, 1956. Herbert and Betty Smith, both California schoolteachers, are confined to iron lungs at Rancho Los Amigos respiratory center in Hondo, California. Their daughters, Jody and Debra, paint Christmas greetings on their mirrors. In October 1955, the Smiths were rushed to a hospital with polio within 18 hours of each other. The National Foundation Ventura County Chapter provided the family more than $16,000 in financial assistance for eight months of hospitalization and nursing care.

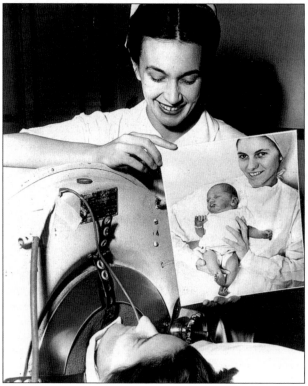

POLIO AND PREGNANCY, JANUARY 21, 1953. Margaret Turner looks at a photograph of her newborn daughter, Patricia, who was born during her confinement to an iron lung. During labor and delivery, Turner was transferred to a small portable respirator. Pregnant women had increased susceptibility to poliovirus, especially during the second half of pregnancy, but the effect on the fetus was more often fatal during early pregnancy. In countries where the incidence of adult poliomyelitis was high, protecting pregnant women became increasingly important.

POOL CLOSED—POLIO, JULY 10, 1953. Polio epidemics tended to occur in summer months, often peaking in August and September. In the attempt to reduce exposure to sources of contagion, health authorities took firm measures to protect the public. The closing of public swimming pools was a common occurrence. Here, the entrance to Brand Memorial Pool in Elmira, New York, bears the warning sign "Closed Polio" in the midst of an epidemic.

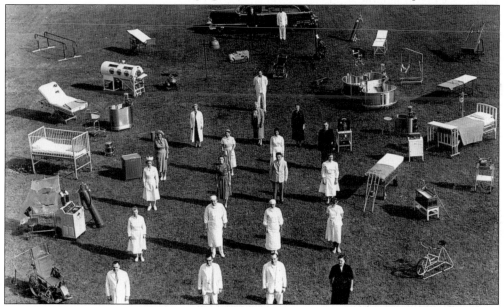

SUPPORT STAFF AND EQUIPMENT, OCTOBER 28, 1955. This is an outdoor view at Grasslands Hospital in Valhalla, New York, depicting the panoply of staff and equipment typically needed by a single polio patient. Staff includes an ambulance driver, ambulance attendant, medical social worker, occupational therapist, nurse, psychologist, pharmacist, x-ray technician, physical therapist, orthopedic surgeon, orthopedic nurse, ear-nose-throat physician, neurologist, anesthetist, and pathologist.

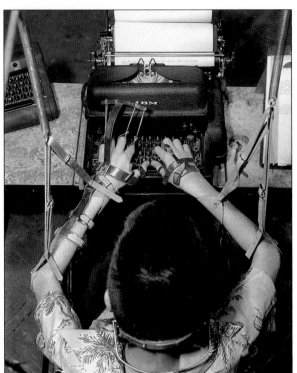

SLINGS AND SPLINTS, C. 1952. Retraining flaccid muscles affected by poliovirus and paralysis was often an arduous process, but it could be accomplished. This young boy from Benton Harbor, Michigan, is learning to type by means of highly customized equipment: a remote-control attachment to an electronic typewriter, a high adjustable lapboard, extension slings for his fingers, and head traction.

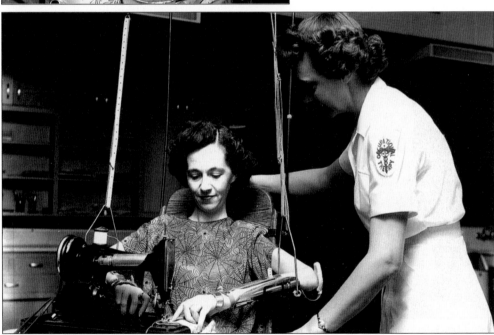

OCCUPATIONAL THERAPY, JUNE 1955. Margaret Thompson, with her arms in suspended splints, works at a sewing machine with an occupational therapist at Rancho Los Amigos in Downey, California. The National Foundation developed not only curricula in occupational therapy to assist in the rehabilitation of the recovering patient but also a program of psychological services to treat depression, a common aftereffect of severe paralysis.

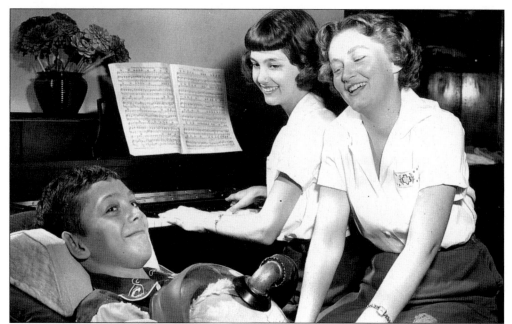

THE WOLFF MEMORIAL HOME, JUNE 1954. Herman Rowland, a patient at the Wolff Memorial Home in Houston, Texas, enjoys music supplied by Girl Scouts Lorelei Ploog and Diane Steele. The Wolff Home served as a comfortable transition between hospital confinement and home residences for the disabled. Mrs. Barney Steele, a Harris County chairwoman for Mothers March on Polio, organized regular weekend visits of Girl Scouts to assist with patient entertainment and socialization. (Courtesy of Edward A. Bourdon.)

THE TUSKEGEE INSTITUTE, OCTOBER 29, 1952. Occupational therapist Ruth Ballard works with Paul Walker at the John A. Andrew Memorial Hospital of the Tuskegee Institute in Tuskegee, Alabama. Founded by Booker T. Washington in 1881, the Tuskegee Institute opened its Infantile Paralysis Center in 1940 through a grant from the National Foundation. Basil O'Connor served as chairman of the Tuskegee Institute Board of Trustees from 1946 to 1968. National Foundation grants to Tuskegee during this period totaled $6.5 million.

POLIO POINTERS, OCTOBER 1951. Led by teacher Rayline Peterson, elementary school children at Walter Allen School in Milwaukee, Wisconsin, read copies of *Polio Pointers*, a National Foundation leaflet. The foundation created and disseminated millions of leaflets, brochures, and other informational literature through the polio era. *Polio Pointers* appeared in several editions and typically recommended "Don't get chilled," "Don't mix with new groups," "Don't get overtired," and similar precautionary messages.

POLIO PRECAUTIONS, AUGUST 1953. Public health advertisements in rapid-transit systems may now seem commonplace, but when the National Foundation Hennepin County Chapter in Minneapolis suggested this step, it was almost a radical idea. The Twin City Rapid Transit Company embraced the polio message wholeheartedly and donated advertising space for 1,150 placards in Minneapolis, St. Paul, Duluth, and Superior. Mrs. James Hannah, chapter educational chairwoman, posts the first *Polio Precautions* advertisement in a Minneapolis trolley.

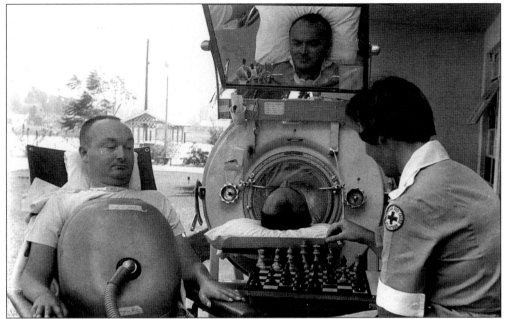

A Chess Game, September 1957. Herman Smith of Ithaca, New York, and Douglas Armstrong of Temple City, California, play chess with the assistance of American Red Cross volunteer Suzanne Errett at Rancho Los Amigos. This match was certainly a triumph of mental fortitude over the personal distress of immobilization, particularly since Armstrong had to strategize and call his moves from a reflection in the mirror on his iron lung.

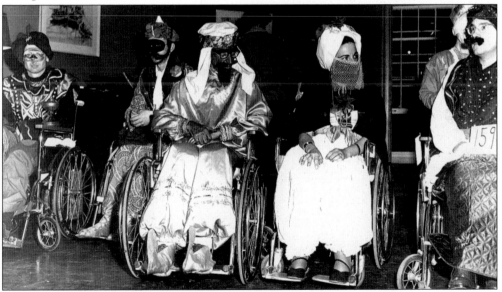

A Halloween Party, 1951. Patients at Georgia Warm Springs embraced a rich tradition of recreational activity with humor and creative engagement. An early Warm Springs patient production in 1936 was titled the *Poliopolitan Opera Company*. Halloween was always an occasion for celebration, and Basil O'Connor once served as a judge for a costume contest. Here, patients in wheelchairs are dressed for a Halloween costume party, possibly depicting the *Arabian Nights Entertainment*.

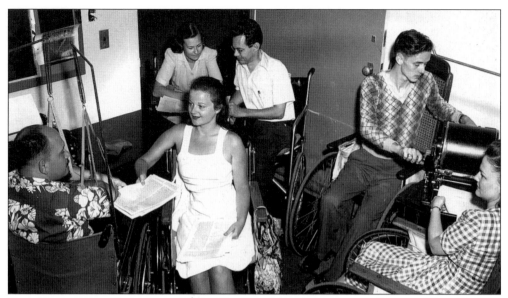

THE WHEELCHAIR REVIEW, C. 1951. The *Wheelchair Review* was a Georgia Warm Springs newsletter written and produced entirely by patients, seen here in the editorial office. Another notable polio-produced newsletter of the 1950s was the *Toomey j Gazette*, named in honor of National Foundation grantee Dr. John Toomey of the Case Western Reserve University School of Medicine. The *Toomey j Gazette* later became the *Rehabilitation Gazette*, produced by Gini Laurie, a founder of the independent living movement.

RUTH JUDD ELLIS, AUGUST 31, 1950. Ruth Judd Ellis was the national college student chairperson of the National Foundation in 1952. The crutches she holds feature her own hand-painted designs. As a student at the University of Florida in Gainesville, she wrote about her experience with polio and the support of the March of Dimes. Ellis remarked, "Polio strikes whether your skin is black or white . . . and the March of Dimes fights back with you."

Larry McKenzie, 1951. Robert Lawrence (Larry) McKenzie (left), March of Dimes poster child of 1951 from Orleans County, New York, smiles as Basil O'Connor holds a coin collector with the boy's likeness. The foundation first selected a poster child to symbolize its mission in posters and coin collectors in 1946. This gave rise to a tradition of nationwide publicity for each new poster child, who was chosen annually to bring attention to both the debilitating aspects of polio and the successes of recovery.

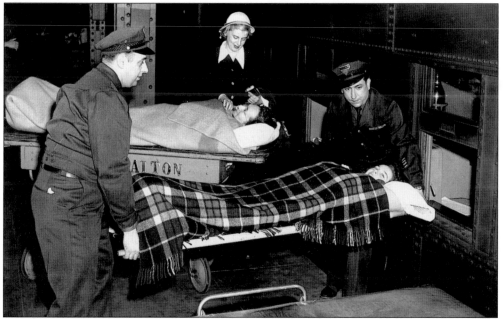

Through Grand Central Station, May 17, 1950. Rita Henderson and Gladys Brewster, neighbors in Barnstead, New Hampshire, are carried on stretchers from the train at Grand Central Station en route to the Georgia Warm Springs Foundation for treatment. The National Foundation Greater New York Chapter made and financed the arrangements for their travel. Brewster commented that she "always wanted to see New York—but not this way."

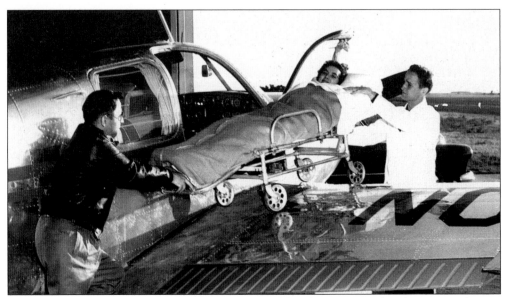

AIR AMBULANCE, 1950. Helen Kitchen, a 21-year-old student nurse with polio at Sacred Heart Hospital in Yankton, South Dakota, is being transferred to Witchita, Kansas, via Air Ambulance. There were many reasons immobilized patients had to travel: when one needed life-sustaining care or advanced treatment, when one was stricken while away from home, or when hospital facilities were overburdened or closed for reconstruction.

MILITARY AIR TRANSPORT SERVICE, 1954. Greta Wilkinson is ferried by a C-54 transport plane from Asheville Orthopedic Hospital in North Carolina to the Respiratory Center of Vanderbilt University in Nashville, Tennessee. Capt. Mary Wyatt checks the patient's condition. The National Foundation developed the Military Air Transport Service (MATS) with the U.S. Air Force for the aerial transport of polio patients throughout the 1950s. Strict, detailed regulations governed the MATS program to guard patient safety and health. (Courtesy of Geraldine Immel.)

AN IRON LUNG PICKUP, 1956. Employees of the National Foundation Cook County Chapter in Chicago unload an iron-lung respirator. Because iron lungs were critical to the survival of patients with respiratory complications, the National Foundation was involved with them from the very beginning. The foundation purchased and loaned iron lungs, evaluated design and functioning, provided training and maintenance, conducted surveys of locations and owners, and created regional equipment pools to stockpile equipment for emergency use.

AN EMERGENCY IN BELGIUM, AUGUST 9, 1949. One of two iron lungs is being loaded on a Pan American World Airways clipper at New York's LaGuardia field for an overseas flight to Brussels, Belgium. In the background, on the tarmac, is a Lockheed Constellation, the first commercial aircraft able to make transcontinental flights in the United States.

A Respiratory Equipment Pool, December 1961. George Tinley adjusts the motor of an Emerson rocking bed at the National Foundation Respiratory Equipment Pool in Augusta, Georgia. The National Foundation and polio patients across the nation relied on the expertise and dedication of employees, volunteers, and many different professionals, including mechanics, who ensured the safe and effective functioning of life-sustaining equipment.

Bettyann Culver, 1950. Bettyann Culver, daughter of Basil O'Connor, was stricken with polio as an adult in July 1950. She poses in this photograph with Dr. Charles E. Irwin (center), medical director and chief surgeon of the Georgia Warm Springs Foundation, and her father. On breaking the tragic news to him, she commented, "Daddy, I've got some of your polio."

A Curb-Climbing Wheelchair, June 17, 1954. Bellevue Hospital instructor Jamie Coffman demonstrates the operation of a curb-climbing wheelchair, designed by New York University engineers under a grant from the National Foundation at the New York University Research Building. Eighteen years before the Federal Highway Act authorized curb ramps in 1972, the foundation was trying to find ways to make streets and sidewalks accessible for the disabled in wheelchairs.

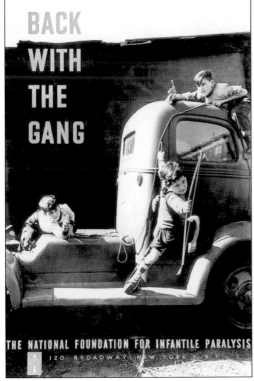

Back with the Gang, 1949. The National Foundation and the Museum of Modern Art in New York commissioned 23 artists in 1949 to create educational posters about polio. *Back with the Gang*, by Helen Leavitt, depicts three young boys playing cops and robbers on a parked truck. The setting is so realistic and the action so natural to energetic boys that one may at first fail to notice that the boy in the foreground wears a leg brace, the very essence of the message that the disabled can and do rejoin the world of the able bodied.

WE POLIOS CAN FILL ALMOST ANY JOB, 1949. Another supremely effective poster in the Museum of Modern Art polio poster contest was *We Polios Can Fill Almost Any Job,* by Milton Wynne. Its message about disability and capability is unmistakable, captured clearly by the portrait of the smiling FDR on crutches in the boy's arms. FDR's legacy as the polio who became president was fixed prominently in the National Foundation's publicity and educational programs about the aftereffects of polio and recovery. The irony in the poster's caption lands squarely on the word "almost." There was no *almost* about FDR. Without question, Franklin D. Roosevelt continues to be a role model of colossal influence not only to the physically disabled but to anyone who faces personal adversity of any kind and accepts responsibility for one's actions to others. In Roosevelt's case, responsibility to others meant his entire constituency—the American people.

Three

MARCH OF DIMES
FUNDRAISING IN ACTION

The March of Dimes was originally the name of the annual fundraising event held each January by the National Foundation for Infantile Paralysis. The story of the origin of the phrase "March of Dimes" itself has a legendary distinction. On November 22, 1937, the comedian Eddie Cantor, in a meeting with Hollywood executives at the Metro-Goldwyn-Mayer studio to discuss fundraising for the new polio foundation, conceived a radio appeal for listeners to send their dimes directly to FDR. He cleverly hit on the phrase "March of Dimes" as a pun on a contemporary newsreel, the *March of Time,* as the name of the appeal. The presidential staff was at first embarrassed by a poor response to the pitch first used in January 1938. Then, the tremendous outpouring of dimes and dollars into the White House mailroom was so enormous that it took months to open the mail and count it all.

The National Foundation scheduled the March of Dimes each January, in keeping with the tradition of observing FDR's birthday on January 30, through the activities of the Committee for the Celebration of the President's Birthday. As that committee waned, the March of Dimes began to stand on its own as the premier fundraising event. Over the years, the foundation marshaled all the resources of mass media—movies, radio, television, newspapers, and magazines—to elicit a furor of concentrated giving. The key ingredient was the appeal to the ordinary person. The campaigns were not geared to gifts from corporations or wealthy philanthropists, but to the American people—the individuals who witnessed the ravages of polio and who placed enormous trust in the foundation that was striving for answers.

The difficulty was keeping the March of Dimes productive and growing year after year. The solution was to place the responsibility into the hands of volunteers. Just as the foundation had developed volunteers for epidemic response, it entrusted fundraising to volunteers who contributed exuberant spirit and fertile imagination to the cause. The plethora of local fundraising devices created by volunteers included parades, exhibits, jingles, square dances, street theater, piggy banks, rummage sales, telethons, polio toll bridges, blue-crutch days, coffee parties, hobo baskets, wheelchair basketball, hay auctions, carnivals, bowling tournaments, and bottle-cap collections. The list goes on and on.

From the silly to the grandiose, from turnip sales and "beans for polio" to Mothers March and high-society fashion shows at the Waldorf-Astoria, March of Dimes fundraising was an integral part of the American scene. Each idea and each dime mattered. The total effect was the creation of a culture of volunteer commitment and sustained giving that transcended the foundation. The March of Dimes represented the generosity of volunteers in every community as the vital spirit of people united in the mission to aid the afflicted and defeat polio.

WHERE ARE YOU FROM, 1945.
An American Red Cross nurse and a member of the Flying Tigers drop their contributions in March of Dimes coin collectors at the U.S. Army airfield in Miami, Florida. After 1945, the National Foundation could no longer depend on the massive movie industry support that it had virtually monopolized during the war years. As movie theater revenue dropped off, the foundation vigorously promoted the annual March of Dimes and related fundraisers.

JACK BENNY'S VAULT, JANUARY 1949. Comedian Jack Benny fostered the impression of being a tightwad, and his vault was a symbol of his penny-pinching obsession. Here, the mayor of Portland, Oregon, Dorothy McCullough Lee, turns the combination lock to the vault, loaded in a covered wagon, during an airplane tour of several cities. The *National Foundation News* reported, "Blood would gush from stones, many believed, long before Benny would part with his well-guarded savings. However, it has finally swung open—for the March of Dimes."

IT'S ALL ABOUT MONEY, 1952. Larry "Turtle" Welch, a radio announcer for WARD radio in Kansas City, Missouri, collected $3,300 during a 100-hour, nonstop fundraiser, playing requests and presenting live musical talent donated by a musician's union to raise money for the 1952 March of Dimes campaign. This photograph appeared in the 1953 *March of Dimes Guide*, an annual planning book for staff and volunteers. (Courtesy of Morton Glosser Studios.)

THE POLIO PARTY LINE, c. 1953. This fundraiser features an improvised stage in the lobby of the Hotel Radisson in Minneapolis, Minnesota. At the microphone with the orchestra is "Harpo" of *Harpo's Bazaar*, a popular local radio program on WCCO radio. Harpo and other radio stars staged this marathon event urging radio listeners to call in pledges to the March of Dimes. Volunteer switchboard operators in the background handled the calls and donations.

THE SUNKIST ORANGE AUCTION, JANUARY 22, 1952. Stuart Strugger and Joyce Fischer conduct bidding for (and on) crates of Sunkist oranges at Hudson River's Pier 21 in New York City. The Tulare County Fruit Exchange of Porterville, California, donated a carload of oranges, and the New York Fruit Auction Corporation waived handling charges and commissions, bringing in a "juicy" $4,000 in proceeds for the March of Dimes. The Sunkist advertisements in the background read, "Mothers! Fresh orange juice comes only in these round packages!"

HELEN HAYES DOLLS, AUGUST 1950. Members of the Monongahela Power Company Girls' Club of Fairmont, West Virginia, display dolls in costumes patterned after those worn by Helen Hayes in various acting roles. Sales of the dolls raised $1,872 for the March of Dimes. Margaret E. Smith, a typist for the company, won first prize for her doll costume creation of *Harriet* (1943), Hayes's Broadway triumph based on the life of Harriet Beecher Stowe. Mrs. Winthrop Rockefeller purchased Smith's *Harriet* for $250. (Courtesy of the Monongahela Power Company.)

CITY HALL, NEW YORK CITY, JANUARY 4, 1954. This is a view of spectators and the stage at the opening rally of the 1954 March of Dimes at city hall in New York City. The slogan "Join the March of Dimes" was a monetary solicitation but one that fostered a sense of participation and belonging by individual contributors who identified with the cause. Basil O'Connor always promoted this sense of identification and democracy in his public speeches and writing by consistently referring to "*your* National Foundation."

A BROADWAY PARADE, JANUARY 15, 1951. A March of Dimes parade on lower Broadway in Manhattan travels south past several notable New York City institutions. On the left are the Horn & Hardart Automat and Child's Restaurant, both famous eateries. On the right, the parade passes the American Telephone and Telegraph Company at the corner of Fulton Street. The scene is just a bit north of National Foundation headquarters on the 11th floor of the Equitable Building at 120 Broadway.

A POLIO BLANKET, 1955. Volunteers carry a March of Dimes polio blanket bearing Mercury dime emblems and measuring 18 by 60 feet in a Seattle, Washington, parade. The blanket may seem a mere postage stamp compared to the AIDS Memorial Quilt of the 1990s, but it was clearly a forerunner in the cause of prevention education during a devastating epidemic. Business-district shoppers and office workers tossed more than $50 into the blanket as it passed by.

MILE O' DIMES, 1955. A 1909 fire truck leads an auto dealer's association parade of 60 vehicles in Hartford, Connecticut. Marquee signs of the *Hartford Courant*, still America's oldest newspaper in continuous publication, advertise, "Help Fight Infantile Paralysis" and "Mile O' Dimes." Established in 1939, Mile O' Dimes was a popular fundraiser that challenged contributors to give enough dimes that would measure one mile when placed end to end. There are 92,160 dimes in one mile, the equivalent of $9,216.

MOTHERS MARCH ON POLIO, 1954. The first house-to-house canvassing in 1947 led to the creation of Mothers March on Polio in 1950 by the Maricopa Chapter in Phoenix, Arizona. Mothers March started with neighborhood solicitations by volunteer mothers. The signature of the campaign was a lighted front porch that indicated willingness to donate. Here, actress Grace Kelly distributes printed literature to Mothers March leaders. Mothers March continues today as a March of Dimes direct-mail campaign.

TONIGHT I AM A MOTHER, JANUARY 29, 1953. Stage and screen stars Raymond Massey and Tyrone Power join Mothers March in Houston, Texas, collecting in mason jars at the home of Mr. and Mrs. Dan C. Smith. Though the leadership of Mothers March was primarily women, male celebrities wearing "Tonight I Am a Mother" badges added a humorous twist used to great effect. National Mothers March chairpersons have included Helen Hayes (1951–1961), Jane Wyatt (1961–1971), and Beverly Sills (1971–1986).

OPERATION BURLEY, DECEMBER 6, 1953. Tobacco in this truck was collected for a March of Dimes tobacco auction on January 30, 1954, in Lexington, Kentucky, with volunteers from local U.S. Marine Corps reservists. The scene is certainly an anachronism in terms of the foundation's present mission. Since the 1960s, the March of Dimes has vigorously supported antismoking initiatives based on evidence that smoking increases the risk of low birthweight and premature birth.

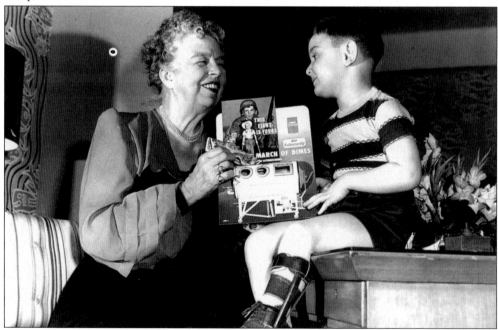

ELEANOR ROOSEVELT, DECEMBER 27, 1951. Eleanor Roosevelt receives a gift of the first 1952 March of Dimes coin collector from Stuart Strugger of the Bronx at the Park Sheraton Hotel in New York City. Eleanor Roosevelt remained a stalwart friend of the National Foundation after FDR's death, campaigning for the March of Dimes, speaking on behalf of the cause, and posing for newsreels and photographs on commemorative occasions. The coin collector, as shown here, was a major fundraising tool.

BOWLING FOR DIMES, MARCH 1953. The fifth annual March of Dimes Bowling Contest was staged in the State Bowling Alleys in Brooklyn, New York, featuring four players of the Brooklyn Dodgers baseball team. They are, from left to right, Gil Hodges, Erv Palica, Eddie Miksis, and Tommy Holmes. Dodgers teammates supported bowling exhibition games and sweepstakes in subsequent years as well. All proceeds supported the March of Dimes.

AN EMERGENCY MARCH OF DIMES, AUGUST 15, 1954. In the years 1949, 1950, and 1954, late-summer polio epidemics depleted National Foundation funds, necessitating special fundraising measures. Basil O'Connor called for an "Emergency March of Dimes" on these three critical occasions to raise additional monies for epidemic relief. This is the opening rally of the Emergency March of Dimes held at Niagara Falls, New York, kicking off a two-week period of fundraising. O'Connor appears in the box at the microphone.

TREVI FOUNTAIN, AUGUST 1954. A replica of Rome's Trevi Fountain serves as a wishing well in Times Square for the 1954 Emergency March of Dimes. Pan American World Airways sponsored the replica. George Redmond watches as Joanne Wilson tosses the first coin over her left shoulder (according to tradition) for good luck. Wishing wells were popular and successful in soliciting the contributions of passersby.

AMERICAN AIRLINES, FEBRUARY 27, 1952. The commercial airlines industry expanded in the 1950s and conspicuously supported the National Foundation. Mrs. Alexander C. Stevens (left) of American Airlines presents Christmas proceeds of its LaGuardia Airport Flagship Desk staff to Beatrice Wright, National Foundation assistant director of women's activities. Bea Wright contracted polio while working as publicity director in Detroit. Behind them is the polio poster *This Fight Is Yours*, by the *Saturday Evening Post* illustrator John Falter.

A FLYING IRON-LUNG BANK, JANUARY 6, 1953. Stuart Strugger and Leslie Strom of the Bronx, along with stewardess Paula Barry of Pelham Manor, New York, make the first contribution to an iron-lung replica at American Airlines terminal, launching it on its 10,000-mile air tour of the United States. The bank raised money in 20 cities for the March of Dimes.

A FLYING VACCINE BOTTLE BANK, JANUARY 4, 1955. Leslie Strom, stewardess Janet Munroe, and David Hill make their contributions to a four-foot polio vaccine bottle replica at the American Airlines terminal in New York. As with the flying iron-lung bank, this one traveled from city to city to raise funds. The method was the same, only the metaphor was different; for polio vaccine and protection against the disease had now become a reality.

CHARLES H. BYNUM, NOVEMBER 14, 1955. Mrs. J.A. Jackson of the Grand Chapter of the Order of the Eastern Star of Virginia presents a $2,000 check to National Foundation director of interracial activities Charles H. Bynum at a March of Dimes pre-campaign meeting in Tuskegee, Alabama. Bynum was a biology teacher and assistant to the president at the Tuskegee Institute before joining the National Foundation in 1944 for a career that spanned three decades of outreach to the African American community.

JAMES "MARCH OF DIMES" JONES, 1955. James Jones of Florence, South Carolina, poses with Clara Mae Thomas and the pickle jar in which he collected $10,000 for the 1956 March of Dimes. Losing a childhood sweetheart to polio in 1938, Jones personally crusaded for the March of Dimes every year, especially during his annual vacation from his job as a railroad redcap on the Atlantic Coast Line. He single-handedly raised more than $231,000 in 30 years of campaigning for the foundation and actually earned the nickname "March of Dimes."

PEANUTS FOR POLIO, 1956. Perry Clark, state chairman of Teens Against Polio (TAP) in Atherton, Kentucky, launches sales in Louisville to commence the Peanuts for Polio project. Teens in other cities also sold lollipops and balloons. Other fundraisers of the time included telethons, iron-lung days, blue-crutch days, auctions, bowling sweepstakes, TAP street sales, and Points for Polio basketball games.

SHELL OUT FOR POLIO, 1956. Here are some quintessential bits of 1950s Americana: Anderson's Rexall drugstore (location unknown), Kodak and Coca-Cola advertisements, teens in short shorts, and the ubiquitous appeal to "Join the March of Dimes." The three girls hold bags of peanuts for sidewalk sales with the sayings "Fight Polio" and "Shell Out for Polio."

METRO PHARMACY, 1954. In the interior of Metro Pharmacy in New York City we find advertisements from Puck Comics and other national advertisers in a nationwide drugstore March of Dimes promotion. Popeye the Sailor, the Katzenjammer Kids, and other cartoon characters appear in a series of advertising banners for Vaseline hair tonic, Band-Aid plastic strips, Super Anahist, Geritol, and, of course, the March of Dimes.

THE 20TH MARCH OF DIMES, 1958. Comedian Eddie Cantor blows out birthday candles to celebrate the 20th anniversary of the March of Dimes. The candles are blue crutches each topped by three tiny dimes. The blue-crutch lapel pin was a popular fundraising device that spawned blue-crutch days. The idea originated with a California Lions Club that purchased the manufacturing dies to make the plastic crutches, selling them for special events.

FATHERS FIGHT FOR MARCH OF DIMES, FEBRUARY 1959. Rudell Stitch of Louisville, Kentucky, assumes a striking pose for a benefit, "Fathers Fight for March of Dimes." Stitch was the No. 2 ranked welterweight boxer in the world in 1960, when he drowned in the Ohio River attempting to rescue a friend. The March of Dimes poster on the right announces the National Foundation's Expanded Program against virus diseases, arthritis, and birth defects in addition to polio. (Courtesy of Gean A. Baron.)

ALL HANDS ON DECK, 1962. Sailors appear in formation, spelling out "March of Dimes" on deck aboard the aircraft carrier USS *Franklin D. Roosevelt*. The ship was the first aircraft carrier named in honor of an American statesman and was in commission from 1945 to 1977. Roosevelt himself was assistant secretary of the navy early in his career. The National Foundation maintained an Armed Forces Division of its Fundraising Department to coordinate regular programs with the military.

THE MARCH OF DIMES FASHION SHOW, JANUARY 28, 1958. Marilyn Monroe appears with poster children Sandra and Linda Solomon at the 14th annual March of Dimes fashion show at the Waldorf-Astoria in New York City. Elaine Whitelaw produced the event from 1945 to 1960 with Eleanor Lambert of the New York Dress Institute Couture Group. Combining fashion pageantry and musical review, the shows introduced designs by Christian Dior, Lilly Dache, Pauline Trigere, and other prominent designers. Luminaries from entertainment, fashion, and high society regularly flocked to the affair. Through the 1950s, Helen Hayes was the national chairperson, and Katherine Chaqueneau was the chairperson of the Patroness Committee. Participants included television panelist Dorothy Kilgallen (*What's My Line?*), Anita Loos (author of *Gentlemen Prefer Blondes*), *Vogue* fashion photographer Cecil Beaton, and artists Alexander Calder and Marcel Vertes. Salvador Dali created stage settings and mobile silhouettes. In 1954, Dali created an armless winged victory statue to symbolize the coming victory over polio. A highlight in 1949 was New York jeweler Harry Winston's collection *The Court of Jewels*.

Four

THE SALK VACCINE FIELD TRIAL OF 1954

From its inception, the National Foundation proceeded with the utmost caution in funding research that would produce realistic, incremental results for the long-term goal of defeating polio. The foundation diligently avoided raising false hopes about a vaccine, after the mistaken efforts in the early 1930s that had plagued the President's Committee on Infantile Paralysis Research. Dr. Jonas Salk, working under a National Foundation grant at the University of Pittsburgh, showed that all strains of poliovirus fell into only three groups. This meant that including a strain from each group would be both necessary and sufficient to make an effective vaccine. At the same time, he began to develop the means to inactivate poliovirus for use in a vaccine. By 1953, it became clear from Salk's initial tests that a polio vaccine for widespread use was feasible and imminent.

After Jonas Salk's successes in immunizing test subjects in Pennsylvania, the National Foundation Committee on Virus Research and Epidemiology endorsed the idea for a nationwide field trial to test the effectiveness of the new vaccine. The foundation organized its Special Advisory Committee on Active Immunization in May 1953 to oversee a plan of action. In November, the foundation formally announced plans for a 1954 field trial of the vaccine in schoolchildren before the start of the summer polio season. The field trial was a massive undertaking that involved the coordinated efforts of the National Institutes of Health, pharmaceutical companies, state and local health officials, medical researchers, and thousands of volunteers.

The field trial of the Salk vaccine was the largest peacetime mobilization of volunteers in American history and was efficiently organized through the foundation's extensive network of county chapters that were active and ready with volunteers. The foundation chose Thomas Francis Jr., M.D., of the University of Michigan at Ann Arbor, to lead an impartial, independent evaluation of the field trial. Francis established the Poliomyelitis Vaccine Evaluation Center. The trial involved nearly two million schoolchildren known as "Polio Pioneers." Francis's announcement on April 12, 1955, that the polio vaccine was "safe, potent, and effective" catapulted Jonas Salk into widespread acclaim. Ultimately, the Salk vaccine reduced the incidence of polio by 96 percent between 1955 and 1961.

The Salk vaccine field trial was but a single brilliant element in the fruition of March of Dimes programs. In 1958, four years after the field trial, the foundation launched its Expanded Program, which included birth defects prevention as a mission component. Planning for this innovation began as early as 1953. The field trial was a resounding success, but it should also be understood as part of a thematic process that encompassed the conquest of polio, advances in genetics, and the development of perinatal health initiatives during the past 50 years.

THE INTERNATIONAL POLIO CONGRESS, SEPTEMBER 3, 1951. The opening ceremony of the Second International Polio Congress in Copenhagen, Denmark, took place in Ceremonial Hall of the University of Copenhagen. Queen Ingrid of Denmark, patroness of the Congress, appears to the left. Basil O'Connor, founder and president of the Congress, became personally acquainted with Dr. Jonas Salk on the return voyage to the United States and forged a friendship with him that would prove critical to the development of the polio vaccine. (Courtesy of Elfelt.)

PRELUDE TO A VACCINE, JANUARY 25, 1952. Leading medical officials discuss the problems of polio at a foundation luncheon at the Carlton Hotel in Washington, D.C. From left to right are Hart van Riper, National Foundation medical director; Leonard A. Scheele, U.S. surgeon general, who holds a pair of leg braces; Basil O'Connor; and Norman Topping, associate director of the National Institutes of Health. (Courtesy of Reni Photos.)

THE COMMITTEE ON VIRUS RESEARCH, 1951. The National Foundation's Committee on Virus Research and Epidemiology, founded in 1938, awarded grants and evaluated progress in poliovirus research. From left to right are the following: (front row) Roger John Williams, Thomas B. Turner, Thomas M. Rivers, and Edward L. Tatum; (back row) Oliver R. Lowry, Joseph E. Smadel, Norman H. Topping, and Leroy E. Burney.

GAMMA GLOBULIN, SEPTEMBER 1953. Gamma globulin is a fraction of human blood that produces passive, and temporary, immunity against disease, including polio. The National Foundation actively supported and funded research into the use of gamma globulin. Here, children and families of Clark and Renick School in Moberly, Missouri, and preschool children from rural areas of Randolph County, stand in line at the city auditorium, waiting their turn for gamma globulin inoculations.

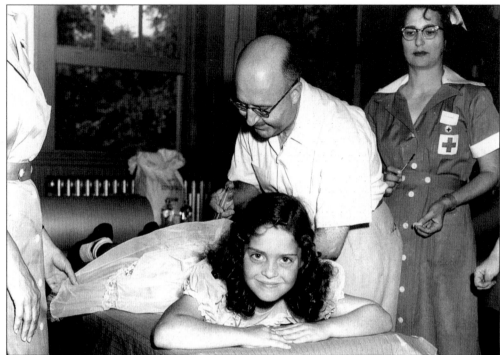

GAMMA GLOBULIN INOCULATION, JULY 1, 1953. Marcia Boyd of Montgomery, Alabama, receives a gamma globulin inoculation from Dr. David Monsky and Eloise Robertson. Field trials of 1951 and 1952 in Utah, Texas, and Iowa, under the direction of National Foundation grantee Dr. William McDowell Hammon, established that gamma globulin produced a short-lived immunity to poliovirus, particularly helpful in summer months during "polio season." In 1953, the foundation orchestrated a mass immunization program of gamma globulin for thousands of schoolchildren.

THE SCIENTIST SPEAKS FOR HIMSELF, MARCH 26, 1953. Basil O'Connor (right) introduces Dr. Jonas Salk to a nationwide audience on the CBS radio special *The Scientist Speaks for Himself.* Salk reported on the vaccine he tested with schoolchildren in Pittsburgh. Two days later, the *Journal of the American Medical Association* published Salk's "Studies in Human Subjects on Active Immunization against Poliomyelitis," in which he first reported techniques of inactivating poliovirus, his injections of 161 individuals, and their antibody responses.

PROGRESS REPORT ON POLIO, 1953. National Foundation officials discuss *Progress Report on Polio* at a chapter workshop meeting in 1953. From left to right are George Voss, director of chapters; Dorothy Ducas, public relations director; Basil O'Connor, president; Elaine Whitelaw, director of women's activities; and Dr. Kenneth Landauer, assistant medical director.

THE VACCINE PRESS CONFERENCE, NOVEMBER 16, 1953. The National Foundation officially announced plans for a vaccine field trial for 1954 at a press conference at the Waldorf-Astoria Hotel in New York City. From left to right are Dr. Hart van Riper, medical director; Basil O'Connor, president; and Dr. Henry Kumm, director of research. Days later, O'Connor met with officials of the Association of State and Territorial Health Officers to outline the administrative and technical details of field trial plans.

RUFUS FITZGERALD AND JONAS SALK, FEBRUARY 1954. University of Pittsburgh chancellor Dr. Rufus H. Fitzgerald (left) and Jonas Salk examine an empty container of trial polio vaccine at the Colfax Elementary School in Pittsburgh, Pennsylvania, where the first inoculations were performed. Salk continued to refine and test his vaccine and to establish manufacturing protocols for pharmaceutical companies, even as field trial plans were under way.

LORRAINE FRIEDMAN, FEBRUARY 1954. Jonas Salk reviews details of the vaccination procedure with his secretary Lorraine Friedman at Colfax Elementary School in Pittsburgh. On the desk in front of them are venules (tubes) marked with children's names for collecting blood samples. In initial tests of his vaccine, Salk carefully administered all vaccinations himself and was adept at putting parents and children at ease. Friedman remained his loyal assistant during his entire career, keeping meticulous records every step of the way.

POLIO PIONEER NO. 1, APRIL 26, 1954. Six-year-old Randy Kerr of Fairfax County, Virginia, became Polio Pioneer No. 1 at 9:35 a.m. on April 26, 1954. He was the first child to be inoculated in the nationwide vaccine field trial. Administering the vaccination is Dr. Richard J. Mulvaney, along with Mrs. Earl Purcell and Mrs. John S. Lucas, at the Franklin Sherman School in McLean, Virginia.

THE VACCINE FIELD TRIAL BEGINS, APRIL 26, 1954. Children at the Franklin Sherman School stand in line waiting for their vaccination at the start of the field trial. The inoculation phase of the trial was conducted in 217 areas of 44 states and 48 additional areas in three Canadian provinces and in Finland. There were 1,831,702 participants. More than 443,000 received one or more inoculations of the vaccine, and more than 210,000 received one or more inoculations of a placebo without significant adverse reactions. The remaining participants were controls.

THE FIELD TRIAL IN NEW YORK CITY, APRIL 27, 1954. Dr. Emanuel Dubow gives an injection to Jeffrey Coles at Public School No. 61 in New York City, as Dr. Leona Baumgartner, Dr. Hart van Riper, and Basil O'Connor look on. By May 4, the New York City Department of Health announced that more than 21,000 children had been vaccinated. Baumgartner praised the work of the 1,600 volunteers recruited by the National Foundation Greater New York Chapter to administer the field trial program in New York City.

ROUNDING THIRD, 1954. This cartoon emphasized that the entire series of three polio vaccine shots was necessary to gain complete protection. The first injection was a sensitizing dose that initiated production of antibodies in the blood. The subsequent two inoculations were booster shots given at appropriate intervals after the primary sensitization. Although sequencing the series of inoculations complicated the administration of the field trial, compliance with the complete series was extremely high.

THOMAS FRANCIS, OCTOBER 1954. Dr. Thomas Francis, director of the Poliomyelitis Vaccine Evaluation Center at the University of Michigan in Ann Arbor, examines the result of a blood test of a child participating in the field trial. He is determining the extent to which antibodies in the child's blood have prevented poliovirus from destroying living cells in the tube mounted on the microscope. The second phase of the field trial ran from June to December, involving an intensive study of blood samples from participating children.

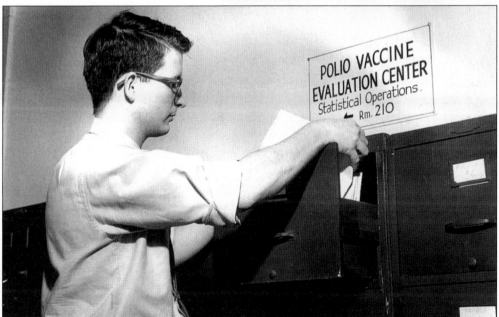

THE POLIO VACCINE EVALUATION CENTER, OCTOBER 1954. The third phase of the field trial required the compilation and evaluation of statistical data to determine whether the vaccine was effective in preventing poliovirus infection. Donald Byrne, U.S. chess master and graduate student at the University of Michigan, retrieves a report on a field trial participant at the Polio Vaccine Evaluation Center. Two years later, Byrne played the 13-year-old Bobby Fischer in a chess match known as "the game of the century."

THE SALK VACCINE ANNOUNCEMENT, APRIL 12, 1955. Dr. Thomas Francis (left), Basil O'Connor (center), and Dr. Jonas Salk discuss the summary report of the Polio Vaccine Field Trial on April 12, 1955, at Rackham Auditorium of the University of Michigan. Francis's announcement that the Salk vaccine was "safe, potent, and effective" represented the culmination of 17 years of intensive efforts by the National Foundation to find an answer to the polio dilemma. The triumphant moment was not lost on the world. News reporters scrambled to get the first word out on the vaccine; communities across the U.S. rang church bells and honked car horns in jubilation; Salk rocketed to immediate and widespread acclaim. Basil O'Connor, too, deserved congratulations, and he got it. One chapter chairman wrote to him, "I realize, and so do thousands of other people, that Dr. Salk discovered the vaccine but without you as the great leader, this could never have been accomplished." However, O'Connor was not one to rest with this monumental accomplishment; he keenly anticipated the logistical and economic difficulties ahead with the vaccination program.

A Presidential Citation, May 1955. Pres. Dwight D. Eisenhower presents Dr. Jonas Salk with a citation commending his work in developing the polio vaccine. Attending the ceremony at the White House Rose Garden in Washington were Salk's family, Basil O'Connor, and Oveta Culp Hobby, U.S. secretary of health, education, and welfare. In 1956, Congress awarded Salk a Congressional Medal of Honor "in recognition and appreciation of his achievement in developing a vaccine for polio."

Needle and Lollipops, May 19, 1955. Allan Stockhouse looks on as Dr. William Geiger prepares the needle at Public School No. 33 in New York City. As soon as the Salk vaccine was licensed, the National Foundation proceeded with an ambitious vaccination program. Approximately five million children received inoculations in April 1955 until the U.S. Public Health Service withdrew the vaccine manufactured by Cutter Laboratories pending investigation of polio cases it had caused. The Cutter incident, however, was only a temporary setback.

THE CHICAGO VACCINATION CLINIC, JULY 1956. Parents and children enter the South Kedzie Avenue Vaccination Clinic in Chicago, Illinois, during an outbreak of polio. Even as the National Foundation took strides to ensure widespread and comprehensive vaccination, polio cases continued to appear and cause suffering. Though the focus was on prevention through vaccination, the National Foundation program of patient aid continued for the time.

TEENS AGAINST POLIO, SEPTEMBER 26, 1956. Mary McLane, national chairwoman of Teens Against Polio (TAP), and Caroline Jackson, Missouri TAP chairwoman, appear at a March of Dimes pre-campaign meeting in Kansas City, Missouri. The National Foundation initiated the Teens Against Polio program to encourage teenagers to get their polio vaccinations and to capture teenage energy for fundraising and programs. (Courtesy of Charles Brenneke.)

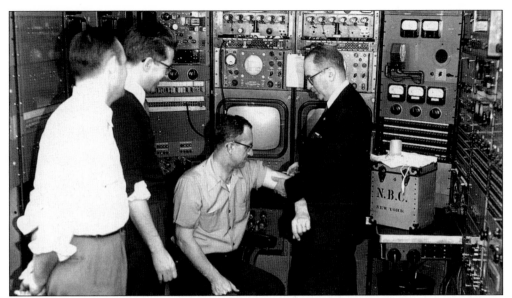

THE EMPIRE STATE BUILDING, MARCH 13, 1957. The National Foundation welcomed every occasion to publicize the vaccination program and sought out photo opportunities in unusual locations, such as this one in the NBC transmission room at the top of the Empire State Building. Dr. Bernard J. Handler, NBC physician, gives a polio vaccination to transmitter engineer George Dlugos, as his colleagues Mathew Bracic and Jerome Stewart of the television antennae crew wait their turns.

POST OFFICE INOCULATIONS, MARCH 11, 1957. By 1957, the foundation found itself in the contradictory situation of having the means to protect against polio and yet still lagging in achieving a 100 percent vaccinated public. Vaccine promotion and education continued throughout the country with health messages, such as "Let's Finish the Job," and mass immunization scenes, such as this one at the main post office terminal in New York City.

POLIO PROTECTION ON PARADE, OCTOBER 1957. A pony pulled this cart of polio-protected youngsters in a Salt Lake City, Utah, street parade. Two television stations brought the vaccination message to more than half a million viewers. As the National Foundation promulgated vaccination, Basil O'Connor exhorted March of Dimes supporters to raise the $44.9 million necessary to continue urgent medical and rehabilitative care for polio patients in 1958.

WHERE WILL POLIO STRIKE NEXT, 1957. This enormous billboard in Chicago's Loop area certainly fulfills the National Foundation imperative of "advertise to immunize." The General Outdoor Advertising Company of Chicago donated the huge advertisement that aided in the city's inoculation efforts. Chicago health commissioner Dr. Herman Bundesen participated for many years in National Foundation activities, beginning in 1940 as chairman of its Committee on Epidemics and Public Health. (Courtesy of Chicago Photographers.)

THE NATION'S LARGEST FAMILY, JANUARY 27, 1957. The nation's largest family turns out for polio shots. Mr. and Mrs. Elmer De Golier of Brockton, New York, with 15 of their 20 children, dramatize the necessity of the polio-prevention program. A National Foundation public health leaflet of the period urged, "Mothers! Dads! Take Your Family for Polio Shots!"

THE NATIONAL HEALTH COUNCIL, 1957. New York City health commissioner Dr. Leona Baumgartner and Basil O'Connor pause in discussion in front of a National Health Council display announcing the National Health Forum of 1958. O'Connor served as president of the council in 1957–1958. Photographs of Baumgartner and O'Connor also appear together in the right-hand panel of the display at the top left.

A MOBILE VACCINATION UNIT, 1959. This is one of two civil-defense vehicles converted to mobile polio vaccination clinics that entered operation on August 4, 1959, in New York City, offering free polio shots. Public health officers in many areas of the country battled public indifference to vaccination with community drives, clinics, and free polio shots.

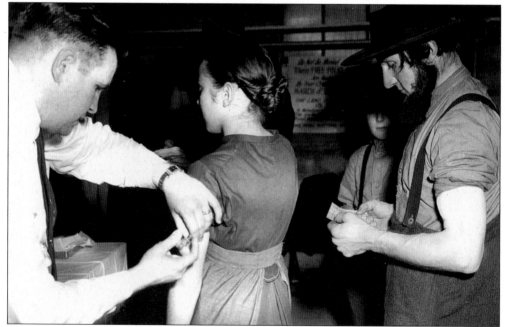

AN AMISH VACCINATION CLINIC, 1959. Dr. Richard K. Chambers gives a polio vaccine injection to 12-year-old Becky Stoltzfus as her brother Benny and father, David, wait their turns at a March of Dimes free vaccination clinic in Georgetown, Pennsylvania. An outbreak of polio in the Georgetown Amish community prompted the group to seek protection, and more than 400 members received their first vaccinations. The last recorded outbreak of polio in the United States occurred in several Midwestern Amish communities in 1979.

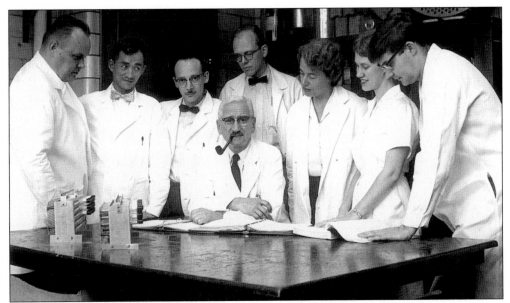

ALBERT SABIN, 1959. Dr. Albert Sabin appears with his research team at the University of Cincinnati in Ohio. Sabin developed a polio vaccine from live, but weakened, strains of the virus, whereas Salk's vaccine was made from the killed, inactivated virus. Sabin and Salk have been portrayed as rivals, but the research of both was crucial to vaccine development and vigorously supported by the National Foundation. By 1961, the foundation had awarded grants to Sabin in excess of $1 million.

THE ORAL POLIO VACCINE, 1960. Dr. Albert Sabin's vaccine could be taken orally in syrup or on a sugar cube, a major advantage over the Salk vaccine that required injection. After mass immunization programs of the Sabin vaccine in Eastern Europe in the late 1950s, the surgeon general recommended licensing the vaccine in the United States. Oral polio vaccine clinics began to supplant vaccination by injection; these became known as Sabin Oral Sundays. The first occurred on April 24, 1960.

SABIN, SALK, AND O'CONNOR, JANUARY 25, 1961. Albert Sabin (left), Jonas Salk (center), and Basil O'Connor appear at an Atlanta Medical Society meeting. This moment of rapprochement belies the testy relationship of Sabin with Salk and O'Connor, especially as the National Foundation worked through the thicket of government agencies and the medical community to make the safest polio vaccine available. It is indisputable, however, that all three men were honest, forthright, and driven by a lifetime commitment to alleviate the human suffering caused by polio. The historian Saul Benison assesses Sabin's work in the following way: even at the height of the Cold War, Sabin's contribution of seed lots of live poliovirus for vaccine in the Soviet Union was applauded "throughout the United States for a humanitarian act that all immediately recognized as being right and just." That Russian scientists accepted this gift on behalf of the Soviet government was also a moment of rapprochement and international collaboration of the highest order. Benison concludes, "That acceptance also stands as measure of the National Foundation's contribution to the conquest of polio."

Five

CELEBRITIES SUPPORT THE MARCH OF DIMES

There is no one so glamorous as a movie star, and the National Foundation had the connections to garner enthusiastic endorsements from major Hollywood celebrities for its polio crusade. The foundation always attracted the best and the brightest from the world of entertainment; in part, this was due to the expectation in the early years that a star *should* contribute to some charitable or humanitarian cause. Though this expectation has diminished over the years, the impact of polio and birth defects has naturally elicited strong support from many quarters, not only from Hollywood and television but also from sports, politics, and the arts. Celebrities who have pitched for the March of Dimes have in many cases made appearances with those captivating icons of popular culture—the March of Dimes poster children, known since 1986 as "special ambassadors" and "national ambassadors."

The person first responsible for the foundation's phenomenal success in utilizing celebrity talent was Howard J. London. London, a talent buyer for a small radio agency, rose quickly to the role of director of the National Foundation's Radio, Television, and Motion Picture Department in the 1940s. Extremely well connected with the agents of celebrities in New York, Chicago, and Los Angeles, he shrewdly orchestrated March of Dimes fundraising campaigns as show business, explicitly intended to entertain. London insisted on dealing only with the top names in entertainment and arranged benefits, tours, radio spots, and movie trailers with stars such as Jack Benny, Doris Day, and Bob Hope. His department also produced informational films about polio and the National Foundation, such as *In Daily Battle* (1946) and *Your Fight against Infantile Paralysis* (1945).

Howard London's successes of the 1940s blossomed into large-scale events, such as the Miss Hush radio contest (Martha Graham was "Miss Hush"), the March of Dimes float in the Tournament of Roses Parade, and the 1956 RCA Starliner Tour. The March of Dimes also reached out to special constituencies, particularly the African American community, through the brilliant path-finding work of Charles H. Bynum, director of interracial activities, and engaged such stars as Sarah Vaughn, Sammy Davis Jr., and Nat "King" Cole. In the very beginning, Basil O'Connor cultivated the participation of Eddie Cantor and Mary Pickford. Some gave their time and talents for decades. These included Helen Hayes, Mary Ann Mobley, Arnold Palmer, and Beverly Sills. In recent years, Daisy Fuentes, Deborah Norville, and Nancy O'Dell have played starring roles in the March of Dimes story. Celebrities have joined the ranks of ordinary Americans to strive together in the singular mission to prevent birth defects and infant mortality, for everyone in this story is a celebrity.

ANN SHERIDAN, JANUARY 29, 1945. Basil O'Connor returns a beguiling smile to actress Ann Sheridan during a dinner associated with a radio broadcast for the 1945 March of Dimes in Boston, Massachusetts. Sheridan, known as "the Oomph Girl," starred in films such as *Naughty but Nice* (1939), *They Drive by Night* (1940), and *King's Row* (1942).

TY COBB AND BABE RUTH, AUGUST 28, 1945. Ty Cobb (left) and Babe Ruth (center) appear with Basil O'Connor at Esquire's All-American Boys Baseball Game at the Polo Grounds in New York City. Ty Cobb served as manager of the West team, and Babe Ruth of the East team. The rivalry between Cobb and Ruth was legendary and intense, and this is one of the rare occasions when they consented to appear together in a photograph.

THE MISS AMERICA PAGEANT, 1949. Contestants in the 1949 Miss America Pageant in Atlantic City, New Jersey, hold a giant March of Dimes polio envelope. Jacque Mercer won the Miss America crown that year. Ten years later, Mary Ann Mobley of Brandon, Mississippi, won the Miss America title, beginning a successful career in film and television and becoming an ardent supporter of the March of Dimes.

EDDIE CANTOR, JANUARY 15, 1951. Comedian Eddie Cantor (left) poses with polio patient Mayreen Hopkins of Brooklyn and Basil O'Connor at National Foundation headquarters. O'Connor appointed Cantor the grand marshal of the Broadway March of Dimes parade that opened the 1951 campaign. Cantor coined the term "March of Dimes" first used in the National Foundation's fundraising drive in 1938 that subsequently became the name of the foundation.

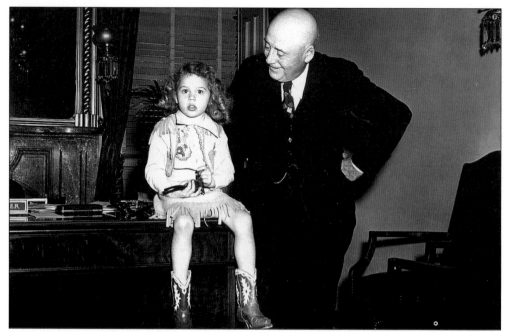

SAM RAYBURN, 1949. Speaker of the House Sam Rayburn talks with 1949 March of Dimes poster girl Linda Brown of San Antonio, Texas. The Texas congressman served for nearly 50 continuous years in the U.S. House of Representatives (1913–1961) as speaker, majority leader, and minority leader. A supporter of FDR's New Deal legislation, Sam Rayburn was known for his impeccable ethics and personal integrity. (Courtesy of Raymond K. Martin.)

RICHARD NIXON, JANUARY 18, 1952. Sen. Richard Nixon of California writes a message of success for the 1952 March of Dimes campaign in the autograph book of poster boy Larry Jim Gross. Nixon had a brief career in the house and senate before serving as vice president under Dwight Eisenhower. In 1955, the National Foundation advertised Nixon's participation in Pumping for Polio Day, in which he pumped gasoline in a Washington gas station.

Bob Considine, November 1954. Sports columnist Bob Considine was named National Sports Council chairman for the 1955 March of Dimes. In 1968, Considine wrote about Basil O'Connor, "All he had going for him was a yellow legal pad, a telephone and a superb knowledge of the business and financial community. Few men he called had the moxie to turn him down, so determined was he to get his partner [FDR] what he wanted for himself and other victims of the cruel and unfathomable disease."

Willie Mays, 1954. Baseball center fielder Willie Mays of the New York Giants goes to bat for the March of Dimes at the Polo Grounds in New York. Known as the "Say Hey Kid," Willie Mays was widely admired for his brilliant playing and showmanship. Many New Yorkers were chagrined when the Giants moved to San Francisco in 1957.

JOHN L. LEWIS, JANUARY 1955. John L. Lewis, president of the United Mine Workers of America (UMWA), adds a dollar to the 1955 March of Dimes for poster girl Mary Koslowski. Lewis, an indisputable hero to U.S. coal miners, served as UMWA president from 1920 to 1960 and helped establish the Congress of Industrial Organizations in the 1930s. The National Foundation regularly cultivated relationships with labor unions for several decades. (Courtesy of Reni Photos.)

LIBERACE, 1954. Pianist and entertainer Liberace presents a check for $2,525 to Frances Karlsteen, executive director of the Cook County Chapter in Illinois. Liberace contributed the entire proceeds of his 1954 concert tour to the Emergency March of Dimes. Such largesse was a measure not only of individual generosity but also of the perception of the urgency and enormity of epidemic polio.

DUKE ELLINGTON, 1952. Pianist, composer, and bandleader Duke Ellington poses with a poster of Randy Donoho of Detroit, Michigan. A towering figure in the history of jazz and American music, Duke Ellington composed in excess of 2,000 songs in his career and produced a host of jazz standards such as "The Mooche," "Sophisticated Lady," "Take the A Train," and "Mood Indigo."

I LOVE LUCY, **FEBRUARY 1, 1954.** Lucille Ball and Desi Arnaz appear with their children Desi IV and Luci Desiree in a special television appeal for the 1954 March of Dimes. *I Love Lucy* was the top-rated television program in the country, and the couple made their pitch to viewers of CBS-TV to send their contributions to the March of Dimes.

FATHER KNOWS BEST, C. 1954. Robert Young and Jane Wyatt of television's *Father Knows Best* pose together for the March of Dimes. Wyatt, who portrayed Margaret Anderson in the series, actively supported the March of Dimes for more than four decades, beginning as development advisor in 1943. She was the second national Mothers March chairperson (1961–1971), the first national chairperson of Volunteer Services (1971–1988), and the first female member of the national board of trustees (1972–1984). She became an honorary trustee in 1984.

MAMIE EISENHOWER, JANUARY 28, 1954. Actress Helen Hayes, "First Lady of the American Theater," presents a scroll of appreciation to Mamie Eisenhower, designating her as "First Lady of the 1954 Mothers March on Polio." Hayes was the first national Mothers March chairperson (1951–1961). First Lady Mamie Eisenhower actively supported Mothers March in 1954 and 1955.

**"SAY, KIDS! WHAT TIME IS IT,"
JANUARY 28, 1955.** Clarabell, the
clown of television's *Howdy Doody
Show*, flashes an ornery smile to the
audience on Doody Dime Day.
Poster girl Mary Koslowski poses
with the puppet Howdy Doody, and
Buffalo Bob Smith beams from the
television screen. The *Howdy Doody
Show* regularly supported the March
of Dimes from 1955 to 1958. Doody
Dime Day in 1955 yielded 300,000
dimes, or $30,000 in proceeds. "It's
Howdy Doody Time!" was also a
time for the unparalleled generosity
of children.

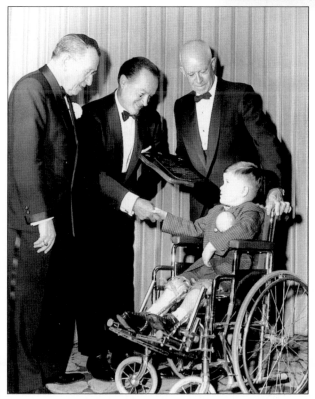

**THE BOB HOPE TRIBUTE
DINNER, MARCH 3, 1961.** The
National Foundation celebrated
the remarkable career of
comedian Bob Hope with a
tribute dinner held at the
Commodore Hotel in New York
City. Basil O'Connor (left)
stands with Hope and Gen. Omar
Bradley as John Maguire, New
York poster boy, presents Hope
with a March of Dimes
Humanitarian Award. In 2003,
Bob Hope celebrated his 100th
birthday. He quipped, "I'm so old,
they've cancelled my blood type."
Thanks for the memories, Bob.

JOHNNY CARSON, AUGUST 23, 1963. In 1967, *Tonight Show* host Johnny Carson received the March of Dimes Man-of-the-Year award. On that occasion, Basil O'Connor wrote, "Like many people with the biggest jobs, Johnny Carson is not too busy to think about sick and handicapped children, not too busy to give of his time and energy to promote the work of the March of Dimes and its fight against birth defects."

RODGER WARD, OCTOBER 18, 1965. Rodger Ward, two-time winner of the Indianapolis 500, poses with March of Dimes poster girl Lori Ann Wagner of Milwaukee, Wisconsin, at the Indianapolis Motor Speedway. A P-38 fighter pilot in World War II, Ward took first place at the Indy in 1959 and 1962. He placed second in 1960 because his tires were worn down to the cords, as Jim Rathmann forged ahead to victory in the final laps.

LEONARD NIMOY, 1968. *Star Trek*'s Spock, Leonard Nimoy, gets an ear pull from March of Dimes poster boy Timmy Faas of Whittier, California. In the *Star Trek* series, Jane Wyatt played Spock's earth mother, Amanda. Nimoy also endorsed the Great American Smokeout in an antismoking poster with the message "Don't Smoke, Live Long and Prosper," accompanied by Spock's Vulcan hand salute.

WILT CHAMBERLAIN AND JERRY WEST, 1969. Basketball champions Wilt Chamberlain and Jerry West pose with poster children Timmy Faas and Loren Beidleman. Chamberlain was known to all as "Wilt the Stilt" of the famed Harlem Globetrotters, and Jerry West was a folk hero in West Virginia for his prowess on the court at West Virginia University. Together, West and Chamberlain were part of the formidable Los Angeles Lakers from 1968 to 1973. (Courtesy of Ralph Gunst.)

CARL STOKES, MAY 1969. Mayor Carl B. Stokes of Cleveland, Ohio, proudly holds Wayne Luising and Valerie Kennerly for Healthy Baby Week. Stokes was the first African American mayor of a major American city. After two terms as mayor (1967–1971), he became the first black news anchorman in New York City. Pres. Bill Clinton appointed him ambassador to the Seychelles in 1994. Stokes died in 1996.

CHARLES MASSEY AND BEVERLY SILLS, 1976. Charles Massey was the third president of the March of Dimes (1978–1989). Here he appears with Beverly Sills and poster boy Robbie Zastavny. Beverly Sills had a brilliant career as soprano and director of the New York City Opera; her involvement with the March of Dimes was also distinguished. She has served as national Mothers March chairwoman (1971–1986), national chairwoman of the 50th anniversary (1987–1988), and as a board-of-trustees member (1989–1993), raising millions of dollars for birth defects prevention.

JOE NAMATH, 1976. Football legend Joe Namath and poster boy Robbie Zastavny display winning smiles. "Broadway Joe," the former New York Jets quarterback, continues to support the March of Dimes enthusiastically as the WalkAmerica honorary celebrity chairman for the Greater New York Chapter (1996–2003). Namath has said, "The March of Dimes is close to my heart—because they are working towards a day when all babies are born healthy and no parent knows the pain of losing a child."

ARNOLD PALMER, 1977. Robbie Zastavny sinks a putt as golf professional Arnold Palmer studies the action. Arnold Palmer served as honorary national chairman of the March of Dimes for more than 20 years and received the foundation's Partner in Science Award. Palmer's support of the foundation stems from personal experience, as his father, Milfred Palmer, recovered from childhood polio. The March of Dimes has sponsored golf events such as the Celebrity Golf Classic and PGA tournaments.

CHRIS EVERT, 1977. Tennis champion Chris Evert assists poster girl Denise Nankivell with her racket. Evert won singles titles in tennis at Wimbledon and the French, Italian, and U.S. opens. She was elected unanimously to the International Tennis Hall of Fame in 1995 and is considered one of the greatest players in the history of tennis.

JIMMY CARTER, 1979. Pres. Jimmy Carter appears with poster child Betsy Burch. Observing the International Year of the Child in 1979, Carter wrote, "In every community of this country the March of Dimes has initiated educational and medical service programs to protect the unborn and the newborn. It has increased the availability of prenatal care, started and supported programs to improve maternal nutrition, created a nationwide group of genetic centers and established and assisted newborn intensive care units."

RONALD REAGAN, 1980. Pres. Ronald Reagan poses with poster girl Melissa Jablonski of Melville, Missouri. On March 23, 1981, the March of Dimes organized a reunion of 33 former poster children at a White House luncheon with Reagan to commemorate the United Nations Year of the Disabled Person. Congressional leaders presented each one with a glass sculpture, "The Protected Child," symbolizing the March of Dimes mission to improve child health by preventing birth defects and improving the outcome of pregnancy.

JAMES BRADY, 1983. James Brady and March of Dimes poster girl Helen Humphrey of Oklahoma City, Oklahoma, give an enthusiastic thumbs-up. Brady was White House press secretary for Pres. Ronald Reagan when they were both wounded in an assassination attempt on the president in 1981. Disabled for life, Brady has gone on to support many initiatives on behalf of the disabled.

CATS ON BROADWAY, 1984. Poet T.S. Eliot meets the March of Dimes in the form of Old Possum's Practical Cats—the stars of the Broadway musical *Cats*. Here, six "gumbie cats" and "jellicles" of Broadway's longest-running musical surround March of Dimes poster girl Kristen Ellis of Hebron, Kentucky. Seen by millions, the show by Andrew Lloyd Webber was a New York institution for 18 years until it closed in 2000.

MARY ANN MOBLEY, APRIL 20, 1987. Miss America of 1959, Mary Ann Mobley, visits an intensive-care nursery. Mary Ann Mobley's career has encompassed television, movies, and filmmaking. In 1965, she starred with Elvis Presley in *Harum Scarum* and *Girl Happy*. Mobley has vigorously supported the March of Dimes in several capacities, as celebrity ambassador, national Mothers March chairwoman, and a board-of-trustees member.

MALCOLM-JAMAL WARNER, OCTOBER 31, 1987. Malcolm-Jamal Warner (left) played Theo Huxtable on television's enormously popular *Cosby Show* for eight seasons and starred in many films, including *The Tuskegee Airmen.* This photograph was taken in Brooklyn, New York, in association with Warner's participation in the March of Dimes fundraiser, WalkAmerica. Manhattan's World Trade Center appears in the background.

SHERYL SWOOPES-JACKSON, JANUARY 1998. Basketball phenomenon Sheryl Swoopes-Jackson of the Women's National Basketball Association palms the ball during a PSA (public service announcement) shoot for the March of Dimes in San Diego, California. In 1996, she won an Olympic gold medal for the U.S. women's basketball team. As spokesperson for the March of Dimes, Swoopes-Jackson has been both educator and role model in guiding women about how to have a healthy pregnancy and healthy baby.

LOUIS ARMSTRONG, C. 1959. Jazz legend Louis Armstrong and drummer Danny Barcelona play for the March of Dimes. The list of jazz musicians who have pitched for the foundation includes Dave Brubeck, Nat "King" Cole, Ella Fitzgerald, Benny Goodman, Lionel Hampton, Stan Kenton, Charles Mingus, George Shearing, Sarah Vaughn, Paul Whiteman, and Nancy Wilson. Trumpeter Jonah Jones performed many benefit concerts during the 1960s; he was known as "King Louis II" after Louis Armstrong. "Satchmo," however, was *the* king. Some consider him not simply the greatest jazz artist but the greatest musician in American history. From his early classic ensembles, the Hot Fives and the Hot Sevens, to his international hit of 1963, "Hello Dolly," Armstrong defined jazz. Known to jazz aficionados as "Pops," Louis Armstrong also appeared in *The Five Pennies* (1959), a film about jazzman Red Nichols, his New York band called the Five Pennies, and his daughter's struggle with polio. Polio sufferers in the world of jazz have included pianist Horace Parlan and saxophonist David Sanborn.

Six

LEADERS IN MEDICINE AND GENETICS

The most symbolic milestone in the quest to comprehend the mechanisms of genetics remains the determination of the double helical structure of DNA by James D. Watson, Ph.D., and Francis Crick, Ph.D. The entire field of molecular genetics devolves from this breakthrough announced in their classic paper, published in *Nature* in 1953, "A Structure for Deoxyribose Nucleic Acid," written while Watson was working at Cambridge University and supported in part by a March of Dimes fellowship. Watson and Crick shared the Nobel Prize in 1962 with Maurice Wilkins for that work. In addition to Watson, there have been nine Nobel Prize winners who have conducted their research with the direct aid of the March of Dimes: John F. Enders, Ph.D., Thomas Weller, M.D., and Frederick Robbins, M.D. (1954); Linus Pauling, Ph.D. (1954); Max Delbruck, Ph.D. (1969); D. Carleton Gajdusek, M.D. (1976); Joseph L. Goldstein, M.D. (1985); and Edward B. Lewis, Ph.D., and Eric F. Wieschaus, Ph.D. (1995). Many other Nobelists have been associated with the March of Dimes.

As the March of Dimes initiated innovative programs in the fields of birth defects and perinatal health, medical genetics (the study of human diseases that are at least partly genetic in origin) remained central to this enterprise. Victor McKusick, M.D., then professor of medicine at Johns Hopkins University and often called "the dean of American medical genetics," said in 1985 that "the March of Dimes can claim major credit for sponsoring the development of the field of medical genetics during the last quarter century." McKusick was the moving force in the establishment of the annual Short Course in Medical Genetics at the Jackson Laboratory in Bar Harbor, Maine, supported in part by the March of Dimes since 1960. Rapid advancements in genetics have expanded our knowledge of heredity and the causes of disease, and achievements of March of Dimes–funded grantees have ranged from practical solutions for specific genetic disorders to systematic gene mapping. What McKusick envisioned two decades ago as a complete sequence map of the human genetic material was to become a reality in the Human Genome Project.

The 1990s saw an increasing pace of critical genetic breakthroughs by March of Dimes–funded scientists. For example, Stephen T. Warren, Ph.D., of Emory University was part of a team that identified the genetic cause of fragile X syndrome, a common form of mental retardation. Inder Verma, Ph.D., of the Salk Institute for Biological Studies showed in a mouse model that gene therapy could cure hemophilia B, a life-threatening bleeding disorder. The portrait gallery that follows introduces many more men and women associated with the March of Dimes who have been world leaders in medicine and genetics.

JOHN PAUL, C. 1942. Dr. John Rodman Paul of the Yale University School of Medicine was the first polio research grantee of the National Foundation. He and Dr. James Trask established the Yale Poliomyelitis Study Unit in 1931 that pioneered clinical epidemiological studies of polio in small communities, including New Haven, Connecticut. He also served on the National Foundation Committee on Epidemics and Public Health. The map behind Paul depicts poliomyelitis incidence rates in the United States by county.

WENDELL STANLEY, C. 1949. Dr. Wendell Stanley began to unlock the mystery of viruses in the 1930s with his research on tobacco mosaic virus, which he isolated in its crystalline form. The National Foundation supported Stanley's work on both tobacco mosaic virus and poliovirus at his Virus Laboratory at the University of California at Berkeley. Stanley poses here with a copy of Dr. Thomas Rivers's seminal work, *Viral and Rickettsial Infections of Man*, first published in 1948.

JOHN ENDERS AND THOMAS WELLER, NOVEMBER 1954. Dr. John Enders (left), Dr. Thomas H. Weller (right), and Dr. Frederick C. Robbins (not shown here) of the Harvard Medical School together won the Nobel Prize in Physiology or Medicine in 1954 for developing a method of cultivating poliovirus in non-nervous tissue culture. This breakthrough had enormous significance, opening an avenue of research upon which Jonas Salk capitalized to create the first killed-virus polio vaccine in cultures other than nerve tissue.

RUSSELL W. BROWN, NOVEMBER 1954. Dr. Russell W. Brown, director of the George Washington Carver Foundation at the Tuskegee Institute, Alabama, removes a bottle culture of living HeLa cells from an incubator. HeLa cells are those of the first continuously cultured strain of carcinoma, which were derived from a woman who died of cervical cancer in 1951. The cells are a laboratory standard that aided in the development of the polio vaccine. Billions were used in blood tests during the Salk vaccine field trial.

LINUS PAULING, 1955. Dr. Linus Pauling constructs a molecular model at the California Institute of Technology. A National Foundation grantee, Pauling won the Nobel Prize in Chemistry in 1954 for his work on the nature of the molecular bond. His models were not just simple illustrations but were essential to the elucidation of the nature of polypeptide molecules, which join amino acids via peptide bonds. Pauling went on to receive the Nobel Peace Prize in 1962.

MAX DELBRUCK, 1957. Dr. Max Delbruck was a professor of biology at the California Institute of Technology when he shared the Nobel Prize in Physiology or Medicine in 1969 with Alfred Hershey and Salvador Luria. Delbruck was originally an atomic physicist who turned to virology and genetics with research into bacteriophages, viruses that attack bacteria. As a National Foundation grantee, he helped elucidate genetic replication mechanisms in viruses. This photograph is from the Fourth International Poliomyelitis Conference in Geneva, Switzerland.

JOSEF WARKANY, 1959. At Basil O'Connor's request, Dr. Josef Warkany advised the National Foundation about the field of birth defects at a critical juncture in the foundation's history. Warkany was a professor of research pediatrics at the University of Cincinnati College of Medicine and widely respected for his prescient analysis of the prenatal and environmental causes of birth defects. He became the first president of the American Teratology Society, wrote the classic text *Congenital Malformations* (1971), and served on the foundation's Committee on Research-Medical Sciences.

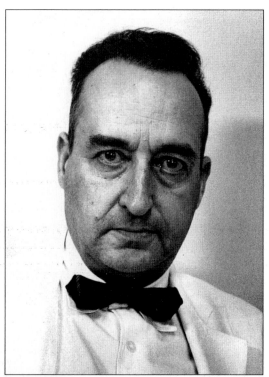

ROBERT GOOD, 1962. Dr. Robert Good studies the x-ray of a thymus gland in his lab at the University of Minnesota. Good, a March of Dimes grantee in arthritis research, demonstrated how the thymus triggers immune reactions in the human body. One of the founders of modern immunology, he identified birth defects related to immune deficiencies and was one of the first to treat birth defects with bone-marrow transplants. Good died in 2003.

ROBERT GUTHRIE, 1963. March of Dimes grantee Dr. Robert Guthrie examines a bacterial inhibition assay test that forms an essential part of newborn screening for phenylketonuria (PKU), an inherited cause of mental retardation. The Guthrie Test is based on the detection of bacterial growth in the presence of abnormally high amounts of the amino acid phenylalanine in the blood. The test can indicate presymptomatic intolerance to phenylalanine in newborns and is a critical tool in preventing this form of mental retardation. All newborn babies receive this test today.

RENATO DULBECCO, C. 1963. Dr. Renato Dulbecco, professor of biology at the California Institute of Technology, became a resident fellow of the Salk Institute. His contributions to virology include the development of the plaque assay method of isolating strains of animal viruses. He discovered that the destructive action of poliovirus on cells created plaques, or films, on the surface of a cell culture. This discovery enabled the accurate quantification of infectious virus particles to determine the virulence of viral strains.

JACOB BRONOWSKI, C. 1963.
Dr. Jacob Bronowski exemplified Jonas Salk's quest for interdisciplinary thinkers at the Salk Institute to fulfill his vision of "bio-philosophy." Bronowski, a senior fellow and later deputy director of the institute, was trained as a mathematician at Cambridge but had a wide-ranging career in government and economics. A polymath who embraced the life sciences and the humanities, Bronowski wrote on quantum physics, algebraic topology, the philosophy of science, and the poetry of William Blake. A key work was his *Science and Human Values* (1956).

DOROTHY HORSTMANN, 1964. Dr. Dorothy Horstmann was a long-term grantee of the National Foundation and the first woman to become a full professor at the Yale University School of Medicine. A member of the Yale Poliomyelitis Study Unit from 1943, she made the key discovery that poliovirus reached the human nervous system via the blood. Here, she studies the Rubella virus, a cause of birth defects (Congenital Rubella Syndrome) in infants whose mothers have had exposure to the virus in early pregnancy.

VICTOR MCKUSICK, C. 1960. Dr. Victor A. McKusick is a pioneer in medical genetics whose work has led to the identification of many inherited genetic disorders and the mapping of the human genome. He founded the Division of Medical Genetics at the Johns Hopkins University and the renowned Short Course in Medical Genetics, sponsored by the March of Dimes at Jackson Laboratory in Bar Harbor, Maine, in 1959.

DANIEL BERGSMA, C. 1965. Dr. Daniel Bergsma was director of professional education for the March of Dimes from 1959 to 1977. He was the creator of the *Birth Defects Atlas and Compendium* (1973) and editor of the *Birth Defects: Original Article Series*. Published from 1965 to 1995, the series was a unique and massive contribution to the birth defects literature with original papers on inherited disorders, gene mapping, embryonic development, and bioethics, as well as proceedings of medical symposia sponsored by the foundation.

ROBERT HOLLEY, OCTOBER 16, 1968. Dr. Robert W. Holley was a resident fellow of the Salk Institute for Biological Studies when he shared the 1968 Nobel Prize in Physiology or Medicine for establishing the nucleotide sequence of ribonucleic acid (RNA). Holley was a professor of biochemistry and molecular biology at Cornell University, where his work on the biosynthesis of proteins led to research on the isolation and structure of RNA.

EZRA DAVIDSON, 1974. Dr. Ezra C. Davidson Jr. is a professor of the Department of Obstetrics and Gynecology at Charles R. Drew University of Medicine and Science in Los Angeles, California. A March of Dimes grantee, his career has encompassed research, education, and public policy on maternal and child health issues. As president of the American College of Obstetricians and Gynecologists (1990–1991), he led a national study of infant mortality and assisted in the creation of the National Fetal Infant Mortality Review Board.

103

SYDNEY GELLIS, 1975. Dr. Sydney S. Gellis was a professor of pediatrics at Tufts University School of Medicine and chairman of the New England Medical Center Hospital in Boston. One of the nation's leading pediatricians, Gellis was chairman of the March of Dimes Basic Research Advisory Committee, which reviews grant applications for research projects on the causes and prevention of birth defects. He also served on the March of Dimes Basil O'Connor Starter Research Advisory Committee and Bioethics Advisory Committee. Gellis died in 2002.

L. JOSEPH BUTTERFIELD, 1975. Dr. L. Joseph Butterfield, a March of Dimes grantee, was chairman of the Department of Perinatology at the Children's Hospital in Denver, Colorado, and a pioneer in the regionalization of perinatal health care. Butterfield led efforts to expand the clinical knowledge of health professionals through coordinated training programs in perinatal health education from Denver to an area that covered major portions of six western states.

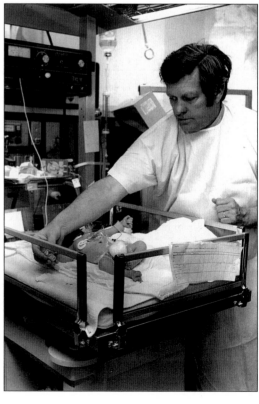

DAVID SMITH, C. 1975. Dr. David Smith, a March of Dimes grantee at the University of Washington in Seattle, was the first to describe and identify fetal alcohol syndrome (FAS) with his colleague Dr. Kenneth Jones. The syndrome describes a wide pattern of physical and mental birth impairments resulting from drinking alcohol during pregnancy. These birth defects are, of course, entirely preventable, and the March of Dimes has produced many educational programs that address the dire consequences that may result from drinking during pregnancy.

DOROTHY AND ORLANDO J. MILLER, 1976. Drs. Dorothy and Orlando J. Miller of Columbia University in New York City developed staining methods for chromosome analysis. Dorothy Miller, a March of Dimes grantee, researched genetic imprinting errors responsible for both birth defects and cancer, and her husband, a cytogenetics expert and professor of obstetrics and gynecology, served for many years on the March of Dimes Basic Research Advisory Committee.

ARTHUR SALISBURY, C. 1978.
Dr. Arthur J. Salisbury was the March of Dimes medical services director from 1970 to 1986 and a leader in the initiative for the regionalization of perinatal care. Under Salisbury's leadership, the March of Dimes Committee on Perinatal Health issued *Toward Improving the Outcome of Pregnancy (TIOP)* in 1976, a landmark publication that led to the restructuring and coordination of maternal and perinatal health care in hospitals throughout the United States.

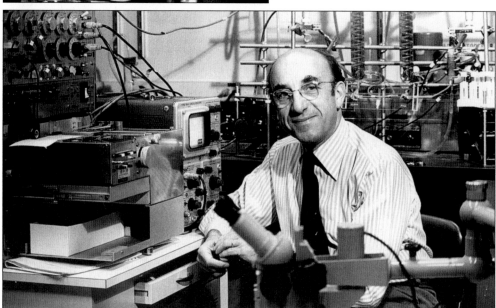

ROGER GUILLEMIN, C. 1978. Dr. Roger Guillemin founded the Laboratories for Neuroendocrinology at the Salk Institute and shared the Nobel Prize in Physiology or Medicine in 1977 with Andrew V. Schally for work on peptide hormone production in the brain. Guillemin's research has enriched our understanding of many processes in cellular physiology and neural biochemistry and has led to improved diagnosis and treatment of thyroid diseases, infertility, and diabetes.

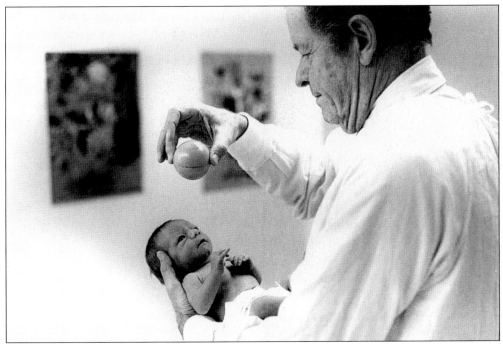

T. BERRY BRAZELTON, DECEMBER 1982. Child development expert Dr. T. Berry Brazelton tests a newborn's perception. An award-winning pediatrician and children's advocate, Brazelton founded the Child Development Unit at Children's Hospital in Boston, Massachusetts. With March of Dimes support, he designed the Neonatal Behavior Assessment Scale that measures the behaviors, coping mechanisms, and capabilities of the newborn infant. Brazelton currently serves on the March of Dimes Board of Advisors.

T. ALLEN MERRITT, C. 1987. Dr. T. Allen Merritt of the University of California San Diego Medical Center helped develop one of the most important breakthroughs relating to respiratory distress syndrome (RDS) in newborns. His surfactant therapy has improved the chances of survival for high-risk, low-birthweight infants jeopardized by respiratory failure. Respiratory difficulties are magnified the more premature the infant is, but surfactant lubricates the lining of the lungs to keep them from collapsing. It is an essential therapy for premature infants with respiratory distress that has dramatically reduced deaths from RDS.

FRANCIS COLLINS, OCTOBER 1999.
Dr. Francis Collins, director of the National Human Genome Research Institute, National Institutes of Health, speaks at the March of Dimes Volunteer Leadership Conference in Washington, D.C. Assisted early in his career with a Basil O'Connor Starter Research grant, he has directed, since 1993, the historic project of creating a complete genetic map of the human genome. Collins stated, "The Basil O'Connor award was a crucial milestone for me, getting me started on a research track that has been intensely gratifying."

SAVIO WOO, JUNE 15, 2000. Dr. Savio Woo speaks at the March of Dimes National Board of Trustees Meeting Retirement Dinner. Woo is the founding director of the Carl Icahn Institute for Gene Therapy and Molecular Medicine at the Mount Sinai School of Medicine in New York City. Formerly a professor of cell biology at Baylor University, he is a widely recognized expert in human genetics and gene therapy.

SYDNEY BRENNER, MAY 6, 2002.
Dr. Sydney Brenner is a distinguished research professor at the Salk Institute in La Jolla, California. One of the foremost biologists of the 20th century, Brenner elucidated the existence and role of messenger RNA in the genetic code and investigated the roundworm *Caenorhabditis elegans* as a model organism in genetics research. He received the March of Dimes Prize in Developmental Biology with Dr. Seymour Benzer (below).

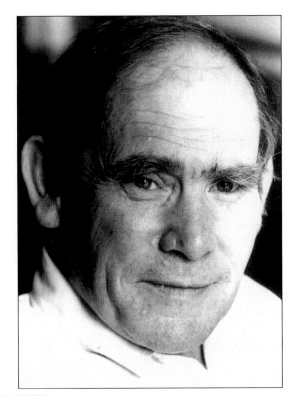

SEYMOUR BENZER, MAY 6, 2002.
Dr. Seymour Benzer is a professor of neurosciences emeritus of the California Institute of Technology. His research into genetics and human development is based on a lifelong investigation of *Drosophila*, the common fruit fly, as a model organism. With Sydney Brenner, Benzer received the Seventh Annual March of Dimes Prize in Developmental Biology in 2002.

VIRGINIA APGAR, C. 1968. If any career typifies the shift from polio to perinatal health, it is that of Dr. Virginia Apgar. After a distinguished career as an obstetric anesthesiologist at the Columbia University College of Physicians and Surgeons, Apgar spent the last 15 years of her remarkable life with the March of Dimes. In 1959, she joined the foundation as director of the newly formed Division of Congenital Malformations. Already well known for the Apgar Score for evaluating newborns, she promoted the development of birth defects registries, campaigned to prevent Rh disease, advocated federal appropriations for rubella immunizations, and traveled constantly as a lecturer, fundraiser, and publicist for the March of Dimes. Apgar never failed to uncover opportunities to focus on the well being of the neonate in the delivery room. Basil O'Connor promoted her to vice president of Medical Affairs in 1968. Her philosophy on prenatal care became an ideal slogan of sound advice to mothers (and fathers): "Be Good To Your Baby Before It Is Born."

Seven

BIRTH DEFECTS
AND PREMATURE BIRTH

In 1958, the National Foundation for Infantile Paralysis launched a new program targeting arthritis and birth defects, with the intention of becoming a "flexible force" in the field of public health. In 1964, the foundation phased out the arthritis component and focused on birth defects, helping to create more than 100 birth defects research and treatment centers across the United States by 1968. Dr. Virginia Apgar, most widely known for the Apgar Score, a system for rapidly assessing the physical condition of newborns, led the foundation's education and prevention campaigns against rubella and Rh disease; both were common causes of major birth defects at the time.

By the 1970s, the foundation's focus expanded to the field of perinatal health. After Basil O'Connor's death in 1972, March of Dimes presidents Joseph Nee and Charles Massey augmented research grants with a clinical grant program and the Basil O'Connor Starter Research grants to encourage promising young investigators. Under their leadership, the foundation developed community programs to improve the health of pregnant women and their infants. In 1976, the March of Dimes led the collaborative Committee on Perinatal Health in producing *Toward Improving the Outcome of Pregnancy* (*TIOP*), a report that recommended nationwide regionalization of perinatal services. *TIOP* is considered a milestone in efforts to put lifesaving technology within reach of every newborn. Support for research on lifesaving advances, such as surfactant therapy for respiratory distress syndrome, advocacy for the creation of a national birth defects surveillance program, and advocacy for screening all newborns for a core list of life-threatening or brain-damaging diseases, are all aspects of the foundation's ongoing mission "to improve the health of babies by preventing birth defects and infant mortality."

The March of Dimes remains a singular, essential American institution that has moved beyond its successes in polio eradication to an unswerving commitment to the health of America's babies. Its programs are wide-ranging because the disturbing realities of birth defects and premature birth require a multi-pronged strategy, from the advanced technology of neonatal intensive care units to advocacy of legislation to expand health insurance coverage for pregnant women and children.

Led by Dr. Jennifer L. Howse as president since 1990, the March of Dimes today is spearheading a national effort to reduce the disturbingly high rate of premature birth and increase awareness of this serious and common problem. The March of Dimes Prematurity Campaign, launched in January 2003, follows the success of the folic acid campaign, which dramatically increased women's awareness that a simple B vitamin, folic acid, can help prevent serious birth defects of the brain and spinal cord. Through research, community services, education, and advocacy, the March of Dimes continues its dedication and service to improve the health of babies.

THE EXPANDED PROGRAM, FEBRUARY 1959. In 1958, the National Foundation unveiled its Expanded Program, which added virus and rheumatic diseases, particularly arthritis, and birth defects as mission components. This giant coin collector of the *new* March of Dimes in New York's Times Square with four locked doors representing four diseases symbolized the expanded mission at the time.

BIRTH DEFECTS CENTERS, 1960. The National Foundation transferred responsibility for arthritis to the Arthritis Foundation in 1964 and began to consolidate its mission around birth defects prevention. One early initiative was the creation of birth defects centers for the diagnosis and treatment of inherited genetic disorders. This is the first Birth Defects Study Center, established at the Children's Hospital in Columbus, Ohio. Dr. Martin Sayers, chief of neurosurgery, links arms with Linda Breese, 1961 poster child, who suffered from spina bifida.

THE SALK INSTITUTE FOR BIOLOGICAL STUDIES, C. 1963. One high-profile project of the 1960s was the creation of the Salk Institute for Biological Studies in La Jolla, California. Designed by architect Louis I. Kahn and financed by the March of Dimes, the Salk Institute opened in 1963 and is considered one of the premier research facilities in the world today, with cutting-edge research in the neurosciences, immunology, cancer biology, and genetics.

JOSEPH NEE, JANUARY 27, 1971. Joseph Nee (right) was the second president of the foundation after O'Connor's death in 1972. He confers with Dr. Vergil Slee of the Commission on Professional and Hospital Activities in Ann Arbor, who demonstrates the computerized detection of birth defects outbreaks. The foundation has also supported the development of state and national birth defects monitoring programs. Today, the March of Dimes manages statistical data on maternal and infant health through the Perinatal Data Center at its national office in White Plains, New York.

THE BOY IN THE BUBBLE, 1973. David Vetter, best known through the media as the "boy in the bubble," represents the mystery and challenge of birth defects. David suffered from severe combined immune deficiency (SCID), a genetic immune disorder that causes uncontrollable susceptibility to infection and disease. Lacking natural immune defenses, he survived only by encapsulation in a bacteria-free environment. David died at age 12, after an unsuccessful bone-marrow-transplant operation.

RUBELLA VACCINATION, 1970. Rubella, or German measles, is a viral disease that, if acquired during pregnancy, may cause a range of birth defects known as congenital rubella syndrome (CRS). These disorders include blindness, deafness, and heart damage. In 1964 and 1965, a major rubella epidemic affected 12.5 million people in the United States, causing 20,000 babies to be born with CRS. The March of Dimes has vigorously promoted protection against rubella through vaccination and education programs.

WINIFRED HOTCH, C. 1969. Winifred "Winnie" Hotch was the Massachusetts state and New England regional volunteer advisor for the March of Dimes. She began her career in 1952 as a Mothers March volunteer and state advisor on women's activities. In 1969, she helped create the first worksite health education program in Massachusetts and on a trip to Italy procured the apostolic blessing of Pope Paul VI on the March of Dimes and its work with the National Council of Catholic Women.

OPERATION STORK, MAY 6–8, 1971. The B'nai B'rith Women and the March of Dimes initiated the prenatal care project Operation Stork in 1968. Alarmed by the fact that many women seek such care for the first time only when they begin labor, the two organizations started their educational outreach to expectant mothers at Grady Memorial Hospital in Atlanta, Georgia. This photograph depicts an Operation Stork health fair at the First Presbyterian Church in Jamaica, Queens, in New York City.

STORK'S NEST, 1971. Stork's Nest is a national, cooperative community service project of the Zeta Phi Beta sorority and the March of Dimes. Like Operation Stork, it began in Atlanta, the scene of this photograph. Since 1971, Stork's Nest has provided educational and referral services for low-income pregnant women. Since early and regular prenatal care is essential to healthy birth, Stork's Nest provides incentives to pregnant women to keep medical appointments and to maintain a healthy diet and lifestyle.

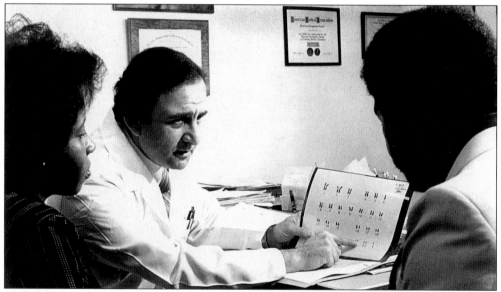

GENETIC COUNSELING, 1978. Dr. Lawrence Shapiro of the Westchester County Medical Center assists a couple in a genetic counseling session. Genetic counselors are health professionals who provide information and support to individuals and families about birth defects and risks for inherited genetic disorders and conditions. The March of Dimes remains a leader in genetics education and support services, from the sponsorship of clinical genetics conferences to developing the *Genetics and Your Practice* curriculum about genetic health care for physicians.

MARTY MIM MACK, 1980. The March of Dimes selected Marty Mim Mack (far left) of Santa Clara, California, as its poster child in 1970. Marty was born without arms, a condition known as phocomelia, and his left leg was shorter than his right. He represented the March of Dimes mission enthusiastically for many years and was named good will ambassador in 1974. Here, he participates in a crew team practice as coxswain.

MARCO CORDOVA, 1980. Marco Cordova, also affected with phocomelia, became the poster child for Monterey County, California, in 1974. Cordova and Mack appeared in the film *Marco and Me* (1981), a production of the March of Dimes and the University of Santa Clara, where Marty was a student. The film depicts Mack's guidance of young Cordova as the two compare how they negotiate their everyday problems. Marco Cordova died in 2001 in a skateboard accident.

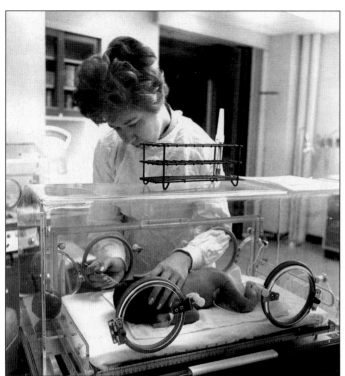

THE NEONATAL INTENSIVE CARE UNIT, 1970. Neonatology, the branch of medicine concerning newborn infants, was born with the development of the incubator in the 19th century. The modern neonatal intensive care unit (NICU) is equipped with an incubator and other sophisticated equipment to treat newborns, especially those born prematurely. Radiant warmers, cardiorespiratory monitors, computerized ventilators, and photo-therapy lights to treat jaundice are some of the essential equipment to be found in a modern NICU.

THE NEONATAL EMERGENCY TRANSPORT INCUBATOR, 1974. A transport incubator is a critical device to transfer a sick or premature infant to life-sustaining medical care. The transport incubator is really a self-contained NICU with built-in respiratory and monitoring equipment. Here, a technician and pilot carry a portable unit to a medical emergency by helicopter.

A MARCH OF DIMES TELETHON, 1969. During the 1960s, a changing economic environment necessitated a reevaluation and redirection of fundraising strategy. The January March of Dimes campaign faded out with the polio era, but the foundation still relied on solid grassroots support. Prior to the advent of WalkAmerica, the organization experimented with many approaches, such as this telethon in 1969 on WLNC-TV in Marquette, Michigan.

PLEDGEWALK, NOVEMBER 1970. The modestly titled "Pledgewalk" caught on in just a few years to become a major fundraiser: WalkAmerica. Here, chapter staff members prepare for the second WalkAmerica event in March of Dimes history in Columbus, Ohio, on November 14, 1970, a few weeks after a similar event in San Antonio, Texas, on October 7. Weather conditions at the Columbus walkathon were "absolutely miserable with rain, cold and bone chilling winds," yet 500 walkers pledged $64,687 to the March of Dimes.

THE NATIONAL TELETHON AGAINST BIRTH DEFECTS, 1984. The March of Dimes presented a nationally televised Independence Day fundraiser each year from 1983 to 1986. The March of Dimes National Telethon against Birth Defects featured actor Hal Linden of the *Barney Miller* television show, Gary Collins of *Hour Magazine*, and actress Mary Ann Mobley. Under the slogan "Let Freedom Ring for America's Babies," mothers-to-be ran through an exercise regime, sending the television audience a message about healthy mothers and healthy babies.

THE CONGRESSIONAL WALKAMERICA, 1983. As WalkAmerica became the mainstay of March of Dimes fundraising, its development included corporate participation through TeamWalk and special events such as the Congressional WalkAmerica. Walking in front are, from left to right, Sen. Ted Kennedy; Arnold Palmer, who carries poster boy Ben Hill; and Speaker of the House "Tip" O'Neill. March of Dimes president Charles Massey appears between Hill and O'Neill.

WALKAMERICA, C. 1993. WalkAmerica remains the premier fundraiser of the March of Dimes. In 1979, the March of Dimes incorporated TeamWalk into the WalkAmerica strategy, inviting participation by teams of employees from other corporations. National corporate sponsors have included Lipton, Kellogg, Kmart, Cigna, and Canon. The event has spawned wraparound events to enhance fundraising opportunities and spin-off events such as WonderWalk and WalkMania.

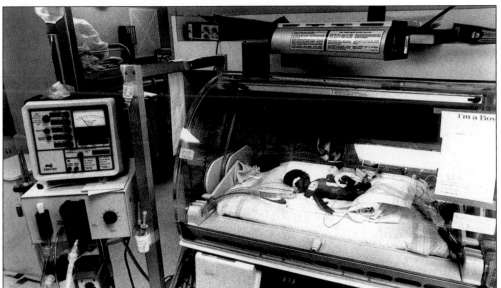

A NEONATAL INTENSIVE CARE UNIT, 1990. This baby, confined to an incubator in a neonatal intensive care unit, was born too soon and too small. Premature babies—those born sooner than 37 weeks of gestation—generally have less-developed organs and can suffer from many lifelong problems, including vision and hearing loss, cerebral palsy, and mental retardation. Some develop bronchopulmonary insufficiency from long-term artificial ventilation. The emotional and physical stress on the families of preemies can transform the joy of birth to an anxiety-ridden experience as the baby struggles for survival in the NICU.

121

BILL CLINTON, 1993. The March of Dimes awarded the Arkansas Citizen of the Year Award to Pres. Bill Clinton and First Lady Hillary Rodham Clinton in 1993. They were the first couple to receive the award. During his presidency, Clinton signed into law two pieces of legislation important to the March of Dimes mission, the Birth Defects Prevention Act of 1998 and the Children's Health Act of 2000. Clinton appears here with March of Dimes national ambassador Jessica Hope Gordon.

JONAS SALK AND JENNIFER L. HOWSE, APRIL 12, 1995. Dr. Jennifer L. Howse (right) is the fourth president of the March of Dimes and the first woman to hold the position. Howse appears here with Dr. Jonas Salk on stage at Rackham Auditorium of the University of Michigan to commemorate the 40th anniversary of the Salk polio vaccine announcement of April 12, 1955. The event honored Jonas Salk and Thomas Francis for their historic achievements in creating and validating the effectiveness of the first vaccine to protect against polio. Salk died just two months later, on June 23, 1995.

JENNIFER L. HOWSE AND INDER VERMA, JUNE 27, 1997. Dr. Jennifer L. Howse, March of Dimes president, visits Dr. Inder Verma, co-director of the Laboratory of Genetics of the Salk Institute in La Jolla, California. Verma is an international authority on the use of viruses in gene therapy and has researched the use of genetically engineered viruses to combat hemophilia, a common bleeding disorder, and other diseases. Howse serves on the board of trustees of the Salk Institute.

GEN. COLIN POWELL, 1997. Gen. Colin L. Powell appears here with March of Dimes national ambassador Cody Groce. The chairman of America's Promise—the Alliance for Youth, Gen. Powell has encouraged March of Dimes youth leaders to expand their leadership potential through volunteerism. In 1998, the March of Dimes pledged $1 million for youth volunteer development as part of its commitment to the America's Promise campaign.

THE FOLIC ACID CAMPAIGN, 1998. Grace Downey and her brother Danny were born healthy, thanks to folic acid. Folic acid, a common B vitamin in certain vegetables and citrus fruits, is a critical nutrient for pregnant women and those planning a pregnancy. In 1998, the March of Dimes launched an educational campaign to encourage women to consume 400 micrograms of folic acid daily before and in early pregnancy to help prevent neural tube defects in the developing fetus, a condition that affects more than 4,000 newborns each year.

THE NATIONAL YOUTH LEADERSHIP CONFERENCE, AUGUST 1998. All smiles and cheers, these participants of the National Youth Leadership Conference at Georgetown University pause during a visit to the Franklin Delano Roosevelt Memorial in Washington, D.C. March of Dimes youth programs encourage volunteerism and community service and foster leadership skills in sexual responsibility and good health practices. Such programs as Team Youth and the National Youth Council foster alliances with other service organizations, giving young people wide-ranging opportunities for creative involvement in life-affirming experiences.

THE DE WAAL INITIATIVE, 2000. The March of Dimes–de Waal mission alliance began in 1999 as a partnership to develop prenatal health education programs in Latin America. With the help of March of Dimes Global Programs, the Dutch-based de Waal Foundation implemented a pilot prenatal health curriculum in Ecuador through its local organization *Proyecto Prenatal*. Here, Quichua women read prenatal literature. The initiative supports the March of Dimes mission to promote improved pregnancy outcomes worldwide.

PROJECT ALPHA, 2000. Project Alpha is a national partnership between the March of Dimes and the Alpha Phi Alpha fraternity, the first Greek-letter fraternity for African American college students in the United States. The Project Alpha program encourages responsible decision making about sexuality, fatherhood, and important life issues through education, role playing, and mentoring. Here, members of the Alpha Phi Alpha national team join the March of Dimes WalkAmerica.

PRES. GEORGE W. BUSH, OCTOBER 11, 2001. Pres. George W. Bush addresses the March of Dimes Volunteer Leadership Conference in Washington, D.C. The catastrophic terrorist attacks of September 11, 2001, nearly resulted in the cancellation of the Volunteer Leadership Conference, an annual event that celebrates the foundation's many dedicated volunteers. Despite the crisis and uncertainty, both the March of Dimes and Bush honored their commitment to be present at this historic event.

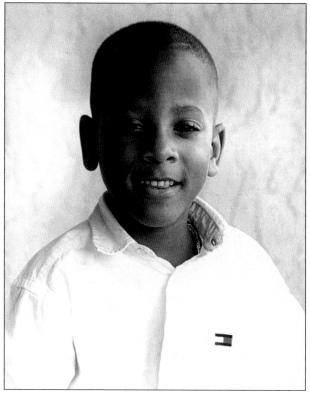

JUSTIN WASHINGTON, 2001. National ambassador Justin Washington represented the March of Dimes for two years, in 2001 and 2002. Justin was born four months premature and weighed only one pound at birth. He underwent corrective surgeries and surfactant therapy, living for weeks on a respirator. Though he overcame a host of physical problems in his first year, Justin is now an irrepressible youngster with comic talents. He and his parents, Dorenda and Kraig Washington, have promoted the March of Dimes mission with great energy in the effort to raise awareness about prematurity.

EMMA HENDERSON, 2002.
National ambassador Emma
Henderson was given only a one-
in-ten chance of survival when she
was born three months premature,
struggling for life in an Oklahoma
City neonatal intensive care unit.
Today, she is an exuberant seven-
year-old who travels the country
with her parents, Susan and Jeff
Henderson, as March of Dimes
ambassadors to share their
experience and educate Americans
about premature birth.

**PRIZE IN DEVELOPMENTAL
BIOLOGY, 2003.** From left to right
are Dr. Ronald M. Evans, Anna
Eleanor Roosevelt, and Dr. Pierre
Chambon. Evans, of the Salk
Institute, and Chambon, of the
College de France, are the recipients
of the eighth annual March of
Dimes Prize in Developmental
Biology. Anna Eleanor Roosevelt is
the granddaughter of March of
Dimes founder Franklin Delano
Roosevelt and has served on the
board of trustees since 1995.

SAVING BABIES, 1979. This nurse at the Jackson Memorial Hospital at the University of Miami, Florida, expresses her care and tenderness for a newborn baby. The photograph originally appeared in the March of Dimes annual report of 1979. The March of Dimes continues the fight for the health of America's children in its various programs to prevent birth defects and infant mortality. The problem of premature birth has assumed epidemic proportions over the two decades since 1981, and no one is working harder than the March of Dimes to find the causes of prematurity and ways to help prevent it. From the very first efforts to eradicate polio with the founding of the National Foundation for Infantile Paralysis in 1938 to the national launch of the Prematurity Campaign in January 2003, the March of Dimes continues to be the premier advocate for maternal and child health in the United States.